TRANSFORMATION: FROM POTENTIAL TO PRACTICE

A HANDBOOK FOR PERSONAL AND ORGANIZATIONAL CHANGE

Edward M. Gurowitz Ph.D.

TRANSFORMATION: FROM POTENTIAL TO PRACTICE

A HANDBOOK FOR PERSONAL AND ORGANIZATIONAL CHANGE

Halo
PUBLISHING
INTERNATIONAL

Halo
PUBLISHING
INTERNATIONAL

Halo Publishing International
7550 W IH-10 #800, PMB 2069,
San Antonio, TX 78229

First Edition, February 2025
ISBN: 978-1-63765-704-1
Library of Congress Control Number: 2024922485

Halo Publishing International is a self-publishing company that publishes adult fiction and non-fiction, children's literature, self-help, spiritual, and faith-based books. We continually strive to help authors reach their publishing goals and provide many different services that help them do so. We do not publish books that are deemed to be politically, religiously, or socially disrespectful, or books that are sexually provocative, including erotica. Halo reserves the right to refuse publication of any manuscript if it is deemed not to be in line with our principles. Do you have a book idea you would like us to consider publishing? Please visit www.halopublishing.com for more information.

To Ed Atkinson—a friend, a mentor,
and a walking master class in transformation.

CONTENTS

WHY TRANSFORMATION?

When I was starting out as a consultant to organizations in the 1980s, the term transformation was not heard in business circles. In fact, the only places it was heard at all were in the blossoming Human Potential Movement in programs such as "est" (Erhard Seminars Training), Lifespring, and others. In business, such talk was considered "woo-woo" and not worthy of consideration. Similarly, terms that are now commonplace in business such as purpose, vision, mission, and values were lumped into the same category.

Today, all these terms are part of the everyday currency of business and industry, and no one blinks an eye at their use, even in "hard" industries such as mining and manufacturing. However, as we will see in the first chapter of this book, many of these terms have been misinterpreted and misunderstood.

I have been working in the area of transformation, both personal and organizational, since the 1970s when I led workshops at Jack Canfield's New England Center for Personal Growth in Amherst. At that time, I brought to participants in the workshops the distinction between being and doing. Increasingly, participants and others at the Center would come to me and say, "You must have done the est Training," which at the time I had barely heard of.

I am a psychologist by degree and at that time I was a psycho-therapist, trained in and practicing a combination of Transactional Analysis, Gestalt Therapy, Family Systems Therapy, and also making a study of Buddhism and other Eastern disciplines.

Around the same time I was doing workshops at the New England Center, I was on the Board of the International Transactional Analysis Association, and as it happened in 1978 I chaired and organized the Association's annual conference which was held in Montreal that year, and a fellow Board member, Herb Hamsher, proposed a workshop at the conference on est and psychotherapy, with Werner Erhard pre-senting. Skeptical to the end, I was taken with Erhard's charisma and in September of 1978 did the est Training in New York City, with Erhard leading a training of five hundred participants. It's a cliché, but it changed the course of my life.

In est, I saw a methodology to bring the opportunity for transfor-mation to people in a way that they could engage with and practice in their lives. Much has been written about est and its successor the Landmark Forum, both their benefits and their shortcomings, and it is not my purpose to go into that here. I saw enough that was positive that, after the Training, I began to participate and in 1981 moved with my family to California and went to work for the organization, first as a project manager (the title was Director) directly for Werner and then as a Trainer and Forum Leader.

In the mid-eighties I worked with Werner and others on redesigning and updating the Training, a project that resulted in the Forum (it was later that it came to be called the Landmark Forum) and in the rede-sign of the Forum from a two-weekend program to one that took three days over one weekend. This led me to a deep dive into the origins of the material of the programs and the nature of transformation itself.

As you'll see, transformation is far from a new idea—it has been around for most of civilization's history—it is a discipline like any other that has tools and concepts to be learned, practices to be carried out, and aspects that must be taken on faith until they become so ingrained that their value is clear. Unlike many (particularly Western) disciplines, transformation can be counterintuitive. As I will explain in the first two chapters, much of how human beings have learned to see the world leads us down developmental paths that are directly opposite to the path of transformation. As Brian Klaas put it in his 2024 book Fluke,"We are organisms, not angels, and our minds are organs, not pipelines to the truth. Our minds evolved by natural selection to solve problems that were life-and-death matters to our ancestors, not to commune with correctness." Our perceptions have been forged over millions of years, fine-tuned to help us survive, nothing more, nothing less.

As we will see, those matters that were "life and death to our ancestors" are the main barrier to transformation in the current age, both for individuals and for organizations.

A few notes for the reader:

- *Nothing in this book is "true." Also, hopefully, nothing is intentionally factually false. Rather what I am attempting here is, first, a comprehensive summary of what we know about transformation at the personal and organizational levels, colored by my experience in working with both individuals and organizations to get them on the path of transformed living.*
- *Where I speak of work I have done with individuals and organizations, I have taken care to mask the identities of those I'm speaking about to respect their privacy.*
- *In another, forthcoming, book I explore religious experience, and distinguish between the experience of Spirit, the sharing of the experience, and institutionalization (not to mention monetization) of those things. Much*

the same can be said of transformation. Many people who have carried the message of transformation have gone on to institutionalize their work and some have become rich from it. It is my intention here to separate the work from the workers. No one has a patent on transformation. It has been around for millennia and comes in many forms with many access points, and I hope to present it in a way that is method-agnostic and let the reader explore methods on their own.

- *Some of the people who have contributed greatly to the development of transformational thinking have aspects of their lives that are problematic. Martin Heidegger, for example, somehow managed to be simultaneously one of the great existential philosophers and a Nazi sympathizer. In the current climate of "cancellation" we risk "throwing the baby out with the bathwater" (discarding value while retaining the superfluous) when we do not separate a person's actions from their thinking. I will note these as they arise, lest the reader think I am ignorant of these cases.*

- *Finally, there is the question of pronouns and other aspects of language that is common, but oppressive. In this book I will try to eschew the cumbersome "he/she" construction and use the plural "they/them/their" unless I mean to refer particularly to people who identify as men or as women. In quoting, particularly from old, male, Caucasian sources, I will take the prerogative of "cleaning up" sexist, racist, or homophobic language. The interested reader can follow the endnotes to the original source.*

CHAPTER ONE
TRANSFORMATION: WHAT IT IS AND WHAT IT ISN'T

We will begin by looking at a common misunderstanding about the nature of transformation—namely, the idea that it is a big or very big revolutionary change. Transformation is very different from change—it is a new way of seeing the world, life, oneself, and others. Consider the definition of the word "change": "to become someone or something different, to alter or modify."

By definition, change is *incremental*—something that already exists is added to, subtracted from, or modified. You could say change takes something known, which currently exists, and produces a new version that is more (or less) like the original and hopefully better.

Evolution, for example, is a process of change over long time periods. We can take almost any species today and through fossil records, DNA analysis, and other methods, trace the steps through which it evolved back through various increments of time.

Looking forward, we can analyze possible modifications to a species, to monetary trends, or to almost any evolving process and guess with a pretty good degree of accuracy how it will change. Depending on the degree to which the process or entity we are studying is stable or chaotic, our ability to predict will be more or less accurate. The systems underlying weather, for example, are fundamentally chaotic, so our ability to predict changes in weather, even with sophisticated data and analysis, is notoriously unreliable. On the other hand, if we look at a building or other structure made of steel and stone, for which the underlying systems are stable, we can make reasonably accurate predictions farther into the future.

Human beings are especially conscious of the vagaries of change, both natural and human induced. Our nervous systems are attuned to change. In fact, we lose awareness of any sensory input that doesn't change (think white noise or pictures on the wall). As we will see later in this book, one particular structure in the brain, the *amygdala* (see chapter two), seems to be designed not only to be sensitive to change, but also to interpret change as a threat and to ready the organism to respond to the threat.

As a result, we humans have become experts on change and have developed a fixation on control. As a scientist, one of the first things I was taught was that the goal of science is *prediction and control.* The word "science" derives from the Latin *scientia*, which means knowledge or knowing, but that ancient meaning quickly gave way to prediction and control, with knowledge seen as the tools needed to achieve this new goal. For centuries, this goal went unquestioned. Those who studied science for knowledge's sake have, in the modern world, come to be derided as "mere theoreticians" and "ivory tower academics." The question every one of those scientific purists comes to loathe is "But what is it good for?"

Said pragmatism, as regards knowledge, has extended to business as well. In business, change means growth, and whole disciplines such as finance, economics, marketing, forecasting, and strategic planning have evolved over the centuries, all with the goal of fostering growth and foreseeing and avoiding anything that might interfere with it.

Yet, as we know and as Brian Klaas illustrates in his book *Fluke: Chance, Chaos, and Why Everything We Do Matters*, no amount of forecasting prowess can defeat nature's way of throwing a spanner in the works[i]. I have no doubt that the buggy-whip industry in the late nineteenth and early twentieth centuries had its prediction wizards who could forecast the demand for buggy whips with great accuracy, as did the wagon and saddle manufacturers. I would be more than surprised to hear that any of those growth experts in 1885, when a German named Karl Benz built what was considered the first modern automobile, predicted the near annihilation of their entire industries.

There is another kind of change that is not incremental or evolutionary, but rather unpredicted and unpredictable (though after any occurrence, there are always so-called experts who say they saw it coming). One term for this type of change is "breakthrough." Another term that has had great currency since the work of Thomas S. Kuhn in his 1962 book *The Structure of Scientific Revolutions* is "paradigm shift." The term capitalizes on the tunnel vision that had the those in the business of supplying and outfitting horse-drawn wagons fail to see that the automobile was coming, or once it came that it was there to stay.

As we will see in chapter three, this business of breakthroughs and paradigm shifts is intimately tied to transformation at the organizational level.

TRANSFORMATION

It is important to be clear that transformation is not change. It's not even BIG change. Transformation is most closely related to Kuhn's paradigm shift idea in that it is an alteration in the very substance of possibility. With transformation, what was considered impossible under the old way of thinking becomes possible, and the unthinkable becomes thinkable.

To understand transformation we must reexamine the very structure of the reality that we were born into, have lived our lives in, and largely take for granted.

One of the most important ideas derived from Einstein's theory of special relativity is that *time* is a dimension of the world, right alongside length, width, and depth. As Klaas puts it, special relativity showed that *when* something happens is as important as *where* it happened. This literally added a new dimension to how we think about history, life, and the present.

Similarly, for thousands of years, human beings have lived as if life were two-dimensional: *doing* and *having*. Other terms for this are "process and content" or "activity and results." Further, those two dimensions are thought to be causally related—what we have is a product of what we do, whether intentionally (I strike a match, causing me to have a fire), unintentionally (I left my raincoat at home, causing me to get soaked in the rain), or even existentially (Descartes's "I think, therefore I am").

In the shadowy recesses of some people's minds, a possible third dimension lurks. For example, how is it possible that two people follow the same steps in making a dish, and one produces a culinary masterpiece, while the other's product is meh? How is it that two equally talented tennis players take the same lessons, use the same equipment, and play under comparable conditions, yet one is a brilliant player while the other is at best okay?

For decades, most people, including my fellow psychologists, thought the answers could be found in—guess what?—the dimensions of doing and having. The superior cook or tennis player *has* talent, *executes* better, *has* a competitive spirit. In psychology, this line of thinking is called "trait theory." Trait theory is an approach to the study of human personality; it is primarily interested in the measurement of traits that can be defined as habitual patterns of behavior, thought, and emotion[ii] that is, patterns of what people do and have.

Some thinkers, however, suspected that there was something else at play, something that, like time, is abstract but exerts a causal influence on the other dimensions. Said another way, ontology, the branch of philosophy that concerns itself with *being* says that *who I am* is as (or more) important as *what I do* and *what results*. For example, every year, thousands of people in the US pay for gym memberships or hire personal trainers. All of those people *do* what athletes do—they buy workout clothes and shoes, they create exercise routines, they practice, etc. All of them *have* what athletes have—the clothes and shoes, the interest in fitness, the gym membership, etc. However, almost none of those people go on to be athletically fit, and even fewer become professional athletes.

If you read interviews with professional athletes—Michael Jordan, Arnold Schwarzenegger, Ronaldinho—one phrase keeps coming up: "I was always [an athlete, a basketball player, a football player]." If you search that phrase on the internet, there are hundreds of hits. To be sure, when they were young, all those star athletes also *did* what the kids did and *had* what they had. But they also had something else: they were *being* athletes from a very young age.

The process of changing from doing and having to actually being is called *becoming*, and it is literally swimming upstream. But to start from being and move naturally through doing and having is to flow with the river, not against it.

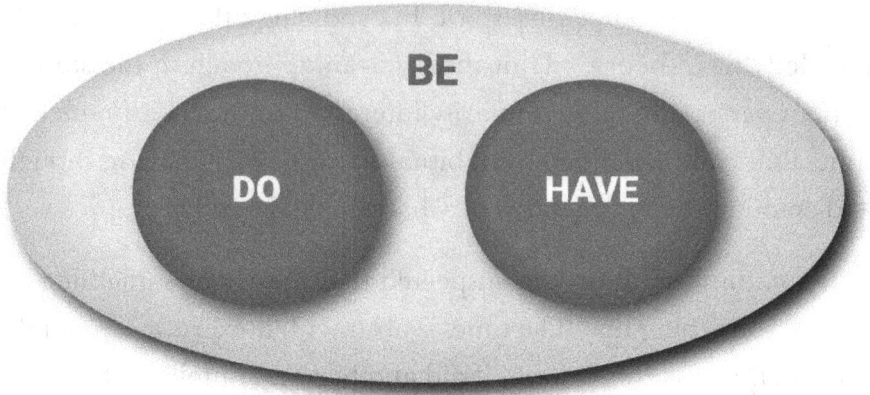

Figure 1

CONTEXT

In this model, *being* functions as a context in which *doing* and *having* occur. Transformation may be defined as *a shift in the locus of identity from content to context*. Said another way, transformation occurs when an entity (a person, a relationship, or an organization) sees itself not as an object or a victim being acted upon by powers greater than itself, but as the space in which the content or circumstances of life occurs.

This is not a new idea—you will find it at the heart of any spiritual discipline, worded according to the terminology of that discipline. Where the differences lie is in how to achieve the transformed state.

The idea of context is not new in science. Early in the nineteenth century, there was a quiet revolution in the still-young field of physics. An English scientist named Michael Faraday (1791–1867), inventor of the electric motor and discoverer of benzene, proposed a remarkable reversal of conventional thinking. That reversal was described by a modern physicist as follows:

> *According to Faraday, rather than looking upon the potential field of force that could be exerted by a bit of matter on other matter...as a secondary derivative property of that matter, one should rather consider the continuous field of potential force as the elementary feature.*

He then viewed the "discrete particle" as a secondary derivative property.

> *According to the field theory proposed, the real stuff of the material world is the abstract (i.e. not directly observable) aspect associated with the potential field of force of matter.*

This view challenged a prevailing philosophical stand, presently known as "naive realism"; it asserts that only that which we human beings directly perceive to be there, outside of us, is the reality from which a true description must follow. Faraday's abstract approach, on the other hand, took the fundamental reality to be at a level underlying that of human precepts.[iii]

It took over a hundred years for the true genius of Faraday's view to be appreciated. It was not until the development of quantum field theory in the 1930s and '40s that physicists began to accept the view that fields might be the "real stuff of the world," to the point that, today:

> *According to quantum field theory, fields alone are real. They are the substance of the universe and not "matter." Matter (particles) is simply the momentary manifestations of*

interacting fields which, intangible and insubstantial as they
are, are the only real things in the universe.[iv]

But what are fields? We cannot observe them directly, even with the most sophisticated of instruments. We recognize them only by their effects. Newton, observing an apple falling from a tree, introduced the field—gravity—which he took to be, as Faraday put it, a secondary derivative property of matter. Later, Einstein postulated that the gravitational field was not a property of matter at all, but the result of space-time curving in response to matter. Thus, for Einstein, gravity was not a force, but a medium, an agency through which something is accomplished.

The other field with which we are most familiar is magnetism, the presence of which we infer from, for example, iron filings lining up in rows instead of scattering themselves randomly. The dictionary defines a field as:

> *An area or division of an activity; the sphere of prac-*
> *tical operation outside a base; a space on which something is*
> *drawn or projected; a region or space in which a given effect*
> *exists; a complex of forces that serve as causative agents in*
> *human behavior; a particular area in which the same type of*
> *information is regularly recorded.*
>
> *Synonyms: realm (as in the realm of science), sphere, prov-*
> *ince, or clearing.*

A prominent modern physicist has said:

> *Although we know a great deal about the way fields affect*
> *the world as we perceive it, the truth is no one really knows*
> *what a field is. The closest we can come to describing what*

they are is to say that they are spatial structures in the fabric of space itself.[v]

For purposes of our work, we can take a probability-based definition of a field as "an area of the world where some things are more likely to happen and/or others are less likely to happen." Thus, in a magnetic field, iron filings are more likely to line up than they are in the absence of such a field. In the gravitational field of Earth, objects are more likely to fall down and less likely to float than they are in outer space, where the gravitational field is weak or nonexistent.

Being, as a field or context, makes certain forms of action (doing) more or less likely. For example, a person who might swear freely in a bar, or at a party with their friends, might refrain from swearing when they are in church or with their grandparents. Context-based behavior is common, and we are often unaware of it, but it is very real.

Where transformation is concerned, it is important to recognize that context may exist by default or by design. As we will see, the default context for human beings is not random or accidental. It is formed by centuries of physical, cognitive, and emotional evolution and is refined for each person by the circumstances of their birth and upbringing. Buddhism was among the earliest philosophies to point this out. Siddhartha Gautama, more commonly known as Buddha, is reputed to have preached that:

- *Life is suffering.*
- *Suffering is caused by attachment.*
- *Suffering can be ended by ending attachment.*
- *The eightfold path (Practices of right view, right resolve, right speech, right conduct, right livelihood, right effort, right mindfulness, and right samadhi (meditative absorption or union) is the way to end attachment.[vi]*

Buddhists believe that the Four Noble Truths, as these are called, both declare the default context and provide a guide to doing what will lead to a new context called "enlightenment" (nirvana). Nirvana, or enlightenment, is an example of a designed context. Unlike default contexts, which accrue with time and experience, designed contexts are created by language.

LANGUAGE

Later in this book, we will examine the role of language in transformation. For purposes of this introduction, it is enough to look at the work of John L. Austin, a British philosopher of language. In 1955, at Harvard, Austin gave a series of lectures called the William James Lectures, later edited and published under the title *How to Do Things with Words.*[vii] He began the lectures by saying:

> *It was for too long the assumption of philosophers that the business of a "statement" can only be to "describe" some state of affairs or to "state some fact," which it must do either truly or falsely. Grammarians, indeed, have regularly pointed out that not all "sentences" are (used in making) statements, also questions and exclamations, and sentences expressing commands or witnesses, or concessions.*

Austin then went on to propose that, in addition to *assertions* of facts, we use language to *do* things, hence the titling of the James lectures as *How to Do Things with Words.* He called this form of language "speech acts."

The philosopher John Searle extended Austin's speech acts and defined these in terms of two factors: "illocutionary force" and "propositional content." The latter is just what it says—the content of an utterance. The former refers to the intent of the utterance—is it a statement, a question, a command, a request, or a promise?[viii] Searle's work was then expanded on by Fernando Flores.[ix]

Designed contexts are created by a particular speech act called "declaration." A declaration is a speech act that creates a context that did not exist until the moment it was declared. For example, two people walk down the aisle and stand before a clergyman, judge, or ship's captain. When they walk up to the officiant, they are both unmarried; after whatever preliminaries are called for (or perhaps with no preliminaries at all), the officiant says, "I pronounce you married," and they walk back down the aisle. As anyone who has been married can tell you, their state of being and the context not only of their relationship but also of their being as persons has changed profoundly. The same can be said of declarations such as "you're hired," "you're fired," etc.

Transformation, then, can be said to be a person's or organization's shift from the default context to a designed context, created by a declaration. In the next chapter, we will examine the default context.

CHAPTER TWO
THE PERFECT STORM

So now that we have clarified the difference between transformation and change, and the nature of transformation itself, what's the problem? People just need to change their mindset or paradigm and—POOF!—they have transformed. So why is it so hard for people to let go of old mindsets, and for society to let go of old paradigms such as racism, sexism, etc.?

The answer is, again, deceptively simple. Just like some people "know" they are athletes or actors, all of us "know" who we are. When confronted with something that requires a transformation to achieve, most of us say, "Yes, I see that would work, but *it's just not me.*" We think we know who we are, and, worse, we think that "who I am" is fixed like a scarab in amber. Beyond that, we see as a threat anything that requires change at a transformational level. In this chapter, we'll see why that is the case.

Some things are innate by design—for example, our eye color is determined by our genes, by the specific combination of DNA that we inherited most immediately from our parents and more remotely from the genetic mix that went into the DNA of our parents, their parents, and on and on, back through generations. The situation is similar for our height, hair color, balding patterns, if any, and myriad other physical characteristics. Other nonphysical things are, arguably, acquired in the course of human development. Yet, experientially, these acquired traits seem as fixed as the physical ones...maybe more so.

In fact, our *identity*—what we refer to when we use the pronoun "I"—is the result of a confluence of factors, or what I call a "perfect storm."

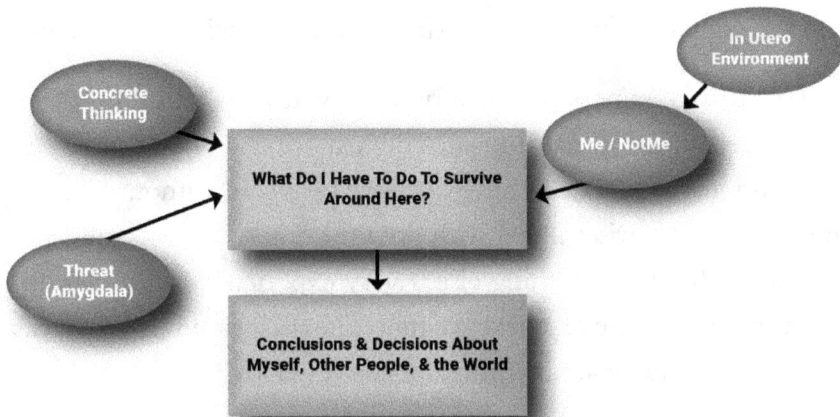

Figure 2

THE IN UTERO ENVIRONMENT AND ME/NOT ME

If we make an educated guess about the world of the fetus before birth, we can surmise that it is an arguably ideal environment— from conception, the fetus is immersed in fluid that is of exactly the temperature of its body, and sound is muted, light diffused. The developing fetus—except in the case of the mother being ill, starving, or killed—never experiences hunger or thirst, pain, pressure, or contact. We can further surmise that, since the nervous system and its associated senses develop gradually over a period of weeks, consciousness dawns gradually and with no sharp transitions.

All this changes almost instantly at birth. Over a very short time, the fetus is subjected to pressure, cold, pain, noise, and light. Most importantly, there is for the first time the experience of *extent*—of having a range over which one extends, of having a surface that is occupied or a distance that is extended over. To be sure, none of these experiences is what we would call cognitive or even conscious; they are more similar to what we experience when leaving a warm bath or swimming pool and the cooler air hits our wet skin—that direct skin-air interface.

This primal experience of a boundary at my skin is likely to have some interesting effects. It locates the experience of self *in the physical body*, and just as you can't have one side of a coin without also having the other, "me" arises along with "not me," and "I" becomes defined in relationship to everything else. Every experience from then on will be within that frame of reference that (a) I am located in my body, and (b) I am separate from anything outside my body.

CONCRETE THINKING

Up until the age of ten or so, a child thinks in absolutely concrete terms. Attributions such as "good girl" or "bad boy" are not heard as situational assessments but as facts. Similarly, and more important for present purposes, "boys don't cry" or "girls don't play with trucks" are not abstract attributions but concrete facts logically equivalent to "you have brown hair." So by the time abstract reasoning begins to develop (and it takes approximately another ten years to develop fully), the child's identity has become fully concretized.

> To the as-yet unborn, to all innocent wisps of undifferentiated nothingness: Watch out for life.
>
> I have caught life. I have come down with life. I was a wisp of undifferentiated nothingness, and then a little peephole

*opened quite suddenly. Light and sound poured in. Voices
began to describe me and my surroundings. Nothing they said
could be appealed. They said I was a boy named Rudolph
Waltz, and that was that. They said the year was 1932,
and that was that. They said I was in Midland City, Ohio,
and that was that.*

*They never shut up. Year after year, they piled detail upon
detail. They do it still. You know what they say now? They
say the year is 1982, and that I am fifty years old.*

Blah blah blah. (Kurt Vonnegut, *Deadeye Dick*)

As schooling and learning take place over the first two decades
of life, the left hemisphere of the brain gets intensive exercise. The
right hemisphere gets less unless the child shows talent in music
or art, when it may get some attention. In her account of a massive
brain hemorrhage in which she temporarily lost the function of her
left hemisphere, the neuroanatomist Jill Bolte Taylor[x] describes the
experience of the right hemisphere as very much like what we surmise
is the experience of the fetus in utero. She calls it "being at one
with the universe" and uses terms such as "I lost the sense of where
I ended and the world began." The left hemisphere, on the other
hand, is conceptual and logical—the home of both concrete and
abstract thinking, in fact thinking at all.

This results in the confluence of attributions that were appre-
hended when only concrete thought was possible and the suppression
of the half of the brain that is capable of experiencing the world as
pure sensation, without boundaries and without words. The identity
becomes simultaneously locked into the physical body, identified in
linear language, located at a point in space called "here" and in time
called "my experience," and into the complex of attributions that are
experienced as qualities of the person.

Attributions are understood to be descriptions, as Vonnegut describes above. Any challenge to "the way I am" becomes a threat to the existence of the identity, and so of the organism itself, with each having the same survival value—if "being nice" or "being smart" is challenged, then I cease to be. Similar cases of self-identification take place regarding race, ethnicity, sexual orientation, and even nationality and regionality.

THE AMYGDALA AND THREAT: HOW THE BRAIN IS COMPLICIT

The oldest structures of the vertebrate brain have looked pretty much the same from the time of the primitive dogfish to humans, All development of the central nervous system occurs through accretion—new structures are added on—and in the case of animals of "higher" intelligence, the greatest accretion is in the development of the hemispheres of the cerebral cortex. But examination of the brain phylogenetically reveals the brain stem does not change much; the amygdala not at all.

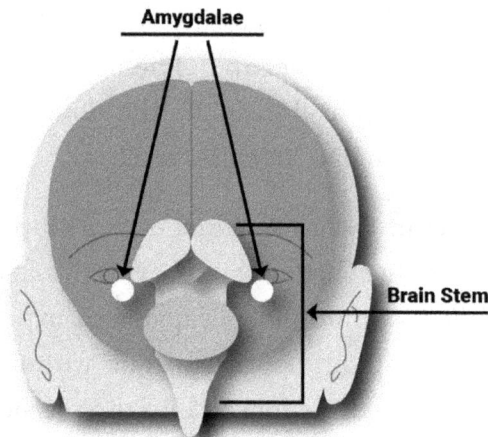

Figure 3: The Human Brain

The key structure in the brain is called the "amygdala" (from the Greek word for "almond," because of its shape). In every species, it has the same function—to detect threat—and it is very good at what it does. Like any good security system, the amygdala is:

- *Fast acting*
- *Highly sensitive*
- *Indiscriminate*

The last of these is critically important for our discussion. The amygdala does not differentiate between real threat, imagined threat, physical threat, social threat, etc. It is designed to ask only one question: Is it safe? In lower animals, the amygdala protects the organism against threats to its life and well-being. As it does in Homo sapiens, but with an added wrinkle: psychological/intellectual development results in the human being identifying the survival of its identity ("who I am") in all its complexity with the survival of the organism, so the amygdala of the human responds to any threat to the identity as if it were a threat to its physical survival.

In other words, if I am an American and you are not, your otherness is a threat to me, and I will respond in the only ways the amygdala allows—by some combination of fighting, fleeing, freezing, or appeasing. Daniel Goleman, in his studies of emotional intelligence, coined the term "amygdala hijack"[xi] to describe what happens when the amygdala is activated by a threat. The amygdala reacts virtually instantaneously; the cerebral cortex, which might discern that what was perceived as a snake is really a stick, takes longer to kick in, and by the time it does, the person will have struck out, fled, frozen in terror, or surrendered.

The addition of the amygdala to the perfect storm creates an interesting effect in human psychology. By virtue of the "me-not me" experience at birth, reinforced by attributions, which continually bombard the developing child with the message that "you are over there, and the world is over here, and you have to find out how to fit into it," human beings increasingly identify themselves as a unique collection of attributes located at a specific point in space and time (commonly called "my point of view").

But an individual's point of view, as we have seen, is not a pure, unadulterated, accurate perception of an objective world. From birth, we accumulate ideas, experiences, and knowledge that act as filters. Because this process begins long before abstract thought, much of this complex of filters is concrete. We experience it not as a point of view, but as "how it is," and lose any sense that our experience is mediated by filters, in much the same way that we can be in an office with tinted windows and think the weather outside is turning bad unless we remember that we are viewing it through darkened glass.

So I don't have a position, a point of view—I am seeing the world as it is. If you see it differently, then you are either misguided, misperceiving, a fool, or a con artist—that is, a threat. It is clear and obvious to me that my perception of the world is more right, better than, and superior to any contrary perception, and the rightness, goodness, and value of any other point of view will be a function of how close it is to mine. Within this framework, the human mind acquires a number of drives, all of which are predicated on my positional view of the world and its primacy. These drives include the certainty that I have exclusive possession of the right worldview (so every other view is, to a greater or lesser extent, wrong). My view must win over and dominate others (so I must avoid losing or being dominated), and it is justified, which invalidates any other view.

This conviction of the rightness of my worldview leads to a situation in which interpersonal exchanges can become competitions for who can convince whom. The word "convince" is important here—it is from the Latin "convincere," to defeat decisively (con: emphasizer; vincere: to defeat). Later, I will propose and explore an alternative—to converse or turn with (con: with; versare: turn)—that is, to see another's point of view.

THE ROLE OF LANGUAGE

Jill Bolte Taylor's recounting of her experience shed light on how astonishingly different the two halves of the brain (called the "cerebral hemispheres") are in their functioning. Her unique experience lent added credence to the idea that the left hemisphere lives in language (in the broadest sense of the word—not English or French or Chinese, but the translation of the world of experience into signs, symbols, and concepts). For the left hemisphere, according to Heidegger, "language is the house of being, in it [humans dwell]."[xii]

Taylor describes the left hemisphere as "preoccupied with details," running her life on a tight schedule, keeping her demeanor serious, and making decisions based on what it learned in the past, defining boundaries and judging everything as good or bad, right or wrong.

The right hemisphere, on the other hand, is all about the present moment, unbridled enthusiasm, and no worries. Early in her book, she describes the first moments after losing the function of her left hemisphere, using terms that will be familiar to anyone who has studied the writings of mystics. Her first experience is of reaching out to steady herself against the wall and being unable to distinguish where "she ended and the wall began." She uses terms such as "at one with the universe" and later describes her "right mind" as filled with gratitude for life and all that is in it, "content, compassionate, nurturing, and eternally optimistic," and goes on to say, "My right mind does not perceive or give heed to territories or artificial boundaries like race or religion."

If, as is our hypothesis, people's relationship to the world begins with a right-hemisphere experience, and if, as seems apparent, the right brain, with its experience of connectedness and intuitive relationship with everyone (and everything), has a driving need to share this experience, the only medium for expressing this experience will be through the left hemisphere, in language. Yet even the best description is doomed to beggar the experience. But for the left brain, description is everything, and that which cannot be described cannot be real. Heidegger noted:

> *To the common comprehension, what is incomprehensible remains forever merely offensive—proof enough to such comprehension, which is convinced it was born comprehending everything, that it is now being imposed upon with an untruth and sham.*[xiii]

The result of this dominance by the left brain is a demand for description and a discounting of that which cannot be described. Teachings are accepted as the communication of experience rather than being known for what they are—the conceptualization and symbolization of that profound experience. If life were a restaurant, the left brain would have us eating the menu instead of the meal.

Experience is thwarted first by the imposition of left hemisphere logic, processional sequencing, and historic bias, but the death blow to experience comes when the description that is adopted is taken as the truth. If what I think is wrong, then I am wrong. My position, the decisions I have made or adopted from others are right, good, and correct; the difference between any other position and mine is a measure of how wrong, bad, and incorrect that position is. So, to return to the amygdala, a threat to my position is a threat to my survival, and it will be met by the amygdaloid responses—fight, flee, freeze, and appease—in some combination. Further, social scientists have been aware for years that groups of like-minded individuals tend to act like individuals—that is, a threat to the group's position will be met with the same ferocity that an individual brings against a threat to their own survival.

"POSITIONALITY"—SYSTEMS AND POLITICS OF IDENTITY

As we have seen, human beings are neurologically and psychologically predisposed to what we will call the illusion of separation. Einstein described this in no uncertain terms:

> *A human being is part of the whole, called by us "Universe," a part limited in time and space. He experiences himself, his thoughts and feelings, as something separated from the rest—a kind of optical delusion of his consciousness. This delusion is a kind of prison for us, restricting us to our personal desires and to affection for a few persons nearest to us. Our task must be to free ourselves from this prison by widening our circle of compassion to embrace all living things and the whole of nature in its beauty. Nobody is able to achieve this completely, but the striving for such achievement is in itself a part of the liberation and a foundation for inner security.* [xiv]

Individual positionality functions not so much as a concept or idea as it does as a context for everything we do. It forms the background for Western thinking and its worldview, filtering what we perceive—it is the default mode of thinking. The act of greeting—of saying hello—in most of the world is an implicit acknowledgment of separateness. We do not begin the day by looking in the mirror and saying hello to ourselves. Greeting is an act reserved for others; "to greet" is a transitive verb; it requires an object. (In more right-brained cultures, greeting can be different from this.) I am over here, you are over there, and I acknowledge your presence.

Humans are social beings. If there were ever a race of solitary humans, its contribution to our gene pool was, at best, minimal. Preservation of the individual in an environment of "nature, red in tooth and claw"[xv] and preservation of the species favored those who could live in groups and groups that could defend themselves against predators, share hunting and gathering responsibilities and, inevitably, defend themselves against other groups who trespassed on their hunting grounds, their settlements, etc.

Just as individual positionality is based in me/not me, tribal positionality is based in us/them. Our way is right, and theirs is wrong; our gods are the true gods, and theirs are false. Our group must survive and thrive. Theirs, not so much—only to the extent that their survival and prosperity does not threaten ours.

The world of what Taylor calls "the right mind" is both harder to describe and equally familiar. We could simply take everything we have said about the left hemisphere and reverse it, but it is worth considering the right hemisphere on its own terms. This is hard to do because we are attempting to do it in language which, as we have seen, is an almost exclusively left-hemisphere function.

But the right hemisphere has a language of its own—it is a language of patterns, rhythms, feelings, intuitions, etc. If we say that for the right hemisphere, there is no time, we are seeing the right-hemisphere experience through a left-hemisphere filter. Rather, we could say that time for the right hemisphere has no past, present, and future. It consists of something we could call "now," but not the momentary now of the left hemisphere—that brief instance of presence that is the bridge between past and future (ignoring the fact that what we call past and future is only experienced in thoughts happening in the present). Rather, the "now" of the right brain is without boundaries and infinite in expanse.

THE EYE OF THE STORM: SURVIVAL

Eric Berne wrote that the fundamental question a very young child has to answer can be metaphorized as "what do I have to do to survive around here?"[xvi] Given what we have learned about the experiential world of the child—positionality, threat, concrete thinking— answering this question is imperative, and it can only be answered with the tools at hand. As a result, it is answered by conclusions and decisions about myself, other people, and the world. These decisions and conclusions are, perforce, negative. In light of the amygdala's constant threat vigilance, the conclusions come in the form of "what's wrong with me, what's wrong with other people, and what's wrong with the world?" The conclusions then form a filter that is the default context of being human, and they form a survival strategy—"In order to survive, I must be…(careful, crafty, the best, smart, etc.)"—which is then elaborated on in the course of growing up.

Thomas Hübl and Julie Jordan Avritt, in their book Healing Collective Trauma, describe this process from the point of view of what they call "developmental trauma," and attribute it to "subjective experiences of shame, humiliation, betrayal, and guilt a child may carry over afterward. Development trauma may include psychological abuse, repeated separation from caregivers, traumatic loss, and exposure to inappropriate sexual behavior."[xvii]

The amygdala is, as we've seen, a highly sensitive threat detector. Any detection system that is used in a high-stakes situation will tolerate what are called "false positives" (registering a threat when there is none) rather than risk "false negatives" (missing a real threat). Given that, while Hübl's developmental traumas may seem dire and rare, in fact even the smallest thing may register as a trauma and trigger defenses of fighting, withdrawing, freezing, or submitting.

Hübl and Avritt also note that even very well-buried traumas may be reactivated as patterns of behavior "from recurring toxic relationship patterns to poisonous social histories. These repetitions are the silent summoning of our unhealed injuries and unexamined failures."[xviii]They point out that Freud cast this phenomenon as "repetition compulsion," an attempt to find conscious resolution to the original trauma.

While the answer to Berne's question—What do I have to do to survive around here?—was formulated in the distant past and with tools that were (a) woefully inadequate and (b) biased toward seeing a threat even when it was not there, transformation, the recontextualizing of the past in the present day, offers a way out of the trap of fixed identity. A reformulation of the self as a new context for one's experience. In the next chapters, we will examine how this can take place for individuals and organizations and how to sustain it.

CHAPTER THREE
PERSONAL TRANSFORMATION

Jimmy was a late arrival in his family, born ten years after his older brother, Frank. There is a folk adage that the first child gets to be whomever they want and the second child gets what's left. Frank, the elder brother, was smart, sociable, well-liked, and athletic from an early age.

Jimmy heard about how great Frank was, and when Jimmy fell short on anything, he heard how Frank did it better. Growing up in a small town, Jimmy went to the same schools as Frank, knew the same people, and in general his perception was that he lived in Frank's shadow. He concluded early on that (a) he would never measure up to Frank, (b) not measuring up was unacceptable, and (c) how to survive was to prove that he was as good as Frank or better. Sociable, well-liked, and athletic were taken, but he could compete on smart. So Jimmy grew up to be known for his intelligence and his readiness to demonstrate his intelligence, including at others' expense. His survival strategy included always making it clear that he was the smartest person in any room he was in.

Also, since part of world of his childhood as he perceived it included that if he did outshine Frank (or the many Frank substitutes he encountered over the years), he would be alone, he developed a sub-strategy of snatching defeat from the jaws of victory. He would excel, then find a way to fail and be re-traumatized, and in recovering, reexperience his ability to survive "not being good enough."

If personal transformation is a matter of shifting one's perspective from the default paradigm that is the survival strategy to a newly created, empowering paradigm, why is it so hard, and why does it take so much time and practice? The answer lies in the deeply embedded conviction that the survival strategy is "who I am." In fact, you've probably said, or heard others say, when confronted with a challenge, "That's just not me," as if what we have called "me" since we were four years old or so is the authentic self. In fact, the "me" is whoever we say it is, and the default sense of self is deeply embedded in survival.

Said another way, the odds are stacked against authenticity for human beings. Whether you believe that the newborn is a tabula rasa or is equipped with preset potentialities, the perfect storm of me/not me concrete thinking and a fully functioning threat detector in the amygdala quickly override whatever the authentic self might be. The developing individual is left with three extremely strong bits of programming: individuation, ego, and suppression/ignorance of being. Add to this the repetition of early trauma and the persistence of the worldview that is comprised of the conclusions and decisions about oneself, other people, and the world, and we are left with the often-heard plaint, "This is how I am."

THE MYTH OF INDIVIDUATION

As we saw in the last chapter, birth brings with it the primal experience of separation. Eminent developmental psychologist Jean Piaget noted that the experience of separateness is a prime aspect of the sensorimotor stage of development (birth to two years).[xix] At the same time, the infant comes to realize that things and people in their environment disappear and reappear, and the notion of "object permanence" develops alongside individuation in the sensorimotor stage. The child comes to know that while other things and people may fluctuate in and out of their experience, the "I" is always there. This is the basis for Einstein's "optical delusion of consciousness" referred to elsewhere in this book.

THE PERSISTENCE OF EGO

Individuation and identity in the form of the survival strategy (see chapter two) develop alongside each other and come to be considered the same. For example, if one of the conclusions that make up the survival strategy is "I'm not smart enough, so I have to prove myself," the cognitive correlate of that will be something akin to "I'm dumb, and nobody better find out, or I won't survive."

Hübl and others consider all of this to be rooted in trauma,[xx] and given the propensity of the amygdala to perceive almost everything as a threat to some degree, this is very likely to be the case. Trauma, however, is only half the story—every trauma was followed by surviving the trauma or threat. Joe Dispenza, an eminent neuroscientist, has written extensively about survival.

> *We unconsciously become addicted to our problems, our unfavorable circumstances, or our unhealthy relationships. We keep these situations in our lives to feed our addiction to survival-oriented emotions so that we can remember who we think we are as a somebody.*[xxi]

Every trauma, every threat has been survived. While much has been written about the impact of trauma and about transcending trauma, survival itself has not received very much attention. I would argue that survival in the face of real or perceived danger is an experience that is powerfully positive. Think about taking a drink of water when you are very thirsty or being released from, say, an MRI machine if you are (like me) extremely claustrophobic. Now multiply that release and pleasure a thousand times. If you have ever been in a life-threatening situation, you will recognize what I am talking about. Survival itself is a massive rush.

Given that experience, it is not, I think, an exaggeration to compare survival to an addictive drug. As we noted in chapter two, the recurrent pattern or re-traumatization seems, in turn, very similar to drug-seeking behavior by an addict. Yes, we repeat trauma, but what we are really repeating is the experience of survival and its concomitant rush.

Jimmy (now Jim) has lived a life of achievement. He earned a doctorate in neuropsychology in just three years, did research, and wrote a book based on his dissertation. He then landed a very good assistant professorship at a university and was well on his way. Two years later, he found himself out of a job—despite being a well-reviewed teacher and being publishing, his colleagues found him argumentative and overbearing, always having to demonstrate his view and that he was smarter than they were.

After a period of time, Jim retrained to become a psychotherapist and went from hospital to private practice, to leading human development workshops all over the world. From there, he moved into organizational psychology as a consultant and founded a successful consulting firm. Falling out with his partners led to his selling his share of the firm and working as a contractor with other consulting firms.

In each of those jobs, he was highly innovative and successful; in each, he managed to offend either colleagues, clients, or both, and leave the firms. One client described him as "high risk, high reward." In one of the firms, he was given a Most Valuable Player award in December and fired in June.

Jim did not understand this pattern very well and created carefully reasoned rationalizations blaming others and circumstances for it.

BLAME: HOW EGO PERSISTS

As we discussed in chapter two, identity or ego has its roots in the perfect storm of positionality, threat, and concrete thinking. Experiences at a very young age lead to what are later realized as conclusions and decisions about oneself, other people, and the world. Given early and incomplete cognitive development, these conclusions and decisions lead to the development of a survival strategy and the view that "I am" a certain way, "other people are" a certain (generally threatening) way, and "the circumstances are" a certain (again threatening) way.

Our early experiential world teaches us that we are objects living in a world of other objects, and we are being acted upon by circumstances that we do not control. In other words, we are victims.

In 1968, Stephen Karpman, a student of Eric Berne, published an article[xxii] to elucidate the mechanism of what Berne, in his seminal book Games People Play,[xxiii] called games. Berne provided a functional or process analysis of various dysfunctional communication patterns (games). Karpman took a structural approach and posited that, regardless of the process of a game, there were always three roles:

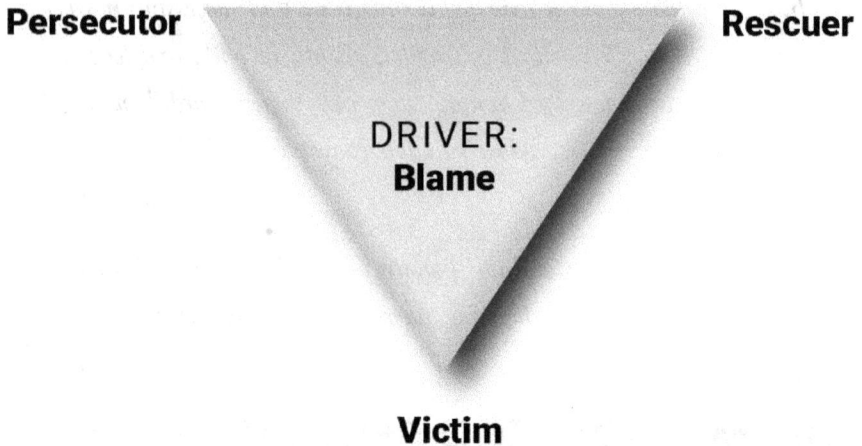

Persecutor   **Rescuer**

DRIVER:
Blame

Victim

Figure 4

Once the roles are established, the game involves switching roles—the nature of the switch defines the nature of the game and creates the drama. While Berne called this "Karpman's triangle," Karpman himself preferred the term "drama triangle," which is mostly how it is known today.

More recent thinking on the Karpman's drama triangle has posited that the glue that holds the dynamic together is blame—the victim blames himself, other people, or the circumstances for his plight; the persecutor blames the victim; and the rescuer seeks to intervene with whomever he blames for the victim's situation.

The drama triangle illustrates a profound and compelling human dynamic. The power in this dynamic is entirely with the victim. As soon as someone becomes the victim, persecutors and/or rescuers will appear. If a rescuer appears, but there's no apparent persecutor on the scene, the victim will sometimes turn on the rescuer ("See—I knew it. You can't help me."), or the rescuer is sucked into the role of persecutor ("You're hopeless—you don't want to be helped.") or victim ("I can't help anyone."). The victim is shown at the bottom of the graphic because, in the end, everyone ends up a victim.

What has been clear to me from the outset is that there is no way out. Awareness will help, and practice will make it harder to get hooked, but in the end, everyone becomes an aware victim. Twelve-step programs have long recognized that the addict (victim) is actually able to stop using, but they continue the dynamic to seek enablers (rescuers) and persecutors.

While there is no way out of the drama triangle, there is an alternative, but it requires, first of all, giving up blame. No more blaming others, the circumstances, or even oneself. This is very difficult to do—blame is integral to the decisions and conclusions that become the underpinnings of every survival strategy. These conclusions and decisions comprise what the early psychiatrist Carl Jung called "the shadow,"[xxiv] which, simply put, means the parts of ourselves that we hide, repress, and deny. The survival strategy operates as an overlay, concealing the shadow from our awareness and that of others (unless you look closely). Similarly, author Brené Brown has written extensively about shame, which she defines as "the intensely painful feeling or experience of believing that we are flawed and therefore unworthy of love and belonging."[xxv] Her definition is comparable to Jung's theory of shadow.

AWARENESS AND ACCOUNTABILITY —THE ANTIDOTE TO BLAME

For the past ten years or so, I've been working on an empowerment model as an alternative to the drama triangle. This model also has three parts:

Confront the Facts

DRIVER:
Accountability

Commitment

Action

Figure 5

It starts with a profound relationship with an unflinching confronting of the facts or data—"What happened is...," **not** "This is what happened to me." Next question: "What is so important to me that I am committed to this situation?" And finally, given these circumstances and my commitment, "What is the appropriate action to take?" (Usually, this will at least be communication.)

In contrast to the drama triangle, which is held together by blame, this dynamic is based on awareness and accountability in the sense that it recognizes that while I may have no choice about what happens to me, I have absolute domain over how I relate to what happens.

Here's the most important part: These two dynamics exist in distinct and nonoverlapping worlds. Said another way, ***there is no blame in accountability, and no accountability in blame.*** One particle of blame—of self, others, or circumstances—is enough to situate a person in the drama triangle. Accountability—accepting or owning what happens, determining or declaring who is committed to being in the matter, and acting on that commitment—is a discipline or a practice. Unfortunately, it's not a fair fight; everything in our wiring—neuropsychologically, psychologically, and culturally—pulls us automatically into the victim mentality, and ***only the practice of accountability can counteract it***.

In all this, self-awareness is key; the quicker I can catch myself in blame—whether as persecutor, rescuer, or victim—the quicker I can move to confronting reality as it is. This move is greatly facilitated by the clear demand to separate data (what happened) from judgment (projection and blame).

In clearing up accountability, the same thing is accomplished by the clear question "Did you keep your agreement?" and the distinguishing of the story, circumstantial explanations, etc. that always involve blame.

AWARENESS 1: FACT VS. INTERPRETATION

In discussing awareness, it is important to distinguish it from knowing. Knowledge and awareness are related concepts, but they have distinct meanings.

Knowledge refers to information, facts, or skills acquired through experience, education, or learning. It involves understanding and familiarity with something, often based on study, research, or personal experience. Knowledge can be explicit, meaning it can be easily articulated and communicated, or tacit, meaning it's more difficult to express explicitly but still influences one's actions and decisions.

Awareness, on the other hand, refers to the consciousness or perception of something. It's the state of being conscious or cognizant of a fact, situation, or phenomenon. Awareness often involves recognizing and understanding the significance or implications of something. It can be more about recognizing one's own thoughts, feelings, and surroundings, as well as the thoughts and feelings of others.

In summary, knowledge is about having information or understanding about something, while awareness is about being conscious or cognizant of that information or understanding, as well as the context and implications surrounding it. Knowledge is often seen as a prerequisite for awareness, as one must have some level of understanding before becoming aware of something.

Jim was a psychologist. Not only had he gone through extensive training, but also his survival strategy required that he learn as much as possible about how the mind works, and he did (and led) a great many personal development workshops. He could even tell you a great deal about his childhood traumas and his survival strategy. He knew but he was not aware.

The victim mindset is pervasive. Philosopher Martin Heidegger coined the term "thrownness"—the idea that we are "thrown" into an "always already" existing world. "People can know the world only because they have in place an implicit understanding, **which is embedded in their coping practices.**"[xxvi]

As we have seen, any threat to the worldview, the survival (or coping) strategy, and implicit victimhood is perceived by the ego as a threat to its and the organism's survival. Awareness, therefore, must be approached gently, with compassion and an eye to distinguishing the "what happened" of a person's childhood from the "what I made it mean."

"What happened" is a matter of facts. The facts of someone's early childhood may be as benign as "my father traveled a lot" or as traumatic as "I watched my father hitting my mother."

Facts are either true or false. A fact must meet three criteria:

1. *Is it real? The opposite is imaginary, something someone told me, etc.*
2. *Is it evident? Is there evidence that it actually existed or had existed. For example, there is evidence that Tyrannosaurus rex existed—we can conclude from that, that they were real. There is no evidence that dragons existed; we cannot, therefore, conclude that they were real.*
3. *Is it demonstrable? Can other people see, hear, smell, or touch it, or am I the only one who can?*

Any phenomenon that meets all three of these criteria will be deemed true or a fact. Any that does not will be false or not factual. It is important to note that no judgment is involved. If something is not a fact, that does not make it bad or wrong; it just puts it into a different category.

If something exists in language but is not a fact, then what is it? It is an interpretation, a conclusion, an inference, an explanation, or any of a number of other language acts. For simplicity, we will lump all these under the umbrella term "interpretation."

An interpretation is always about something that is considered a fact. To ask if an interpretation is true or false, right or wrong, is meaningless. Rather, the test for an interpretation is validity or fit. Does the interpretation fit the facts? If I look at the sky during the setting of the sun (fact) and say it is "beautiful" or "colorful," that is a valid interpretation. If I say it is "obscene" or "dishonest," that interpretation is invalid, not to mention nonsensical.

What happens in early childhood can be said to be put into a system that does not understand abstraction, and so it understands everything as facts. Further, everything and anything can trigger the amygdala's threat response, and so the interpretation of the facts becomes colored by threat, and conclusions are drawn. Those conclusions become the survival strategy based on a worldview consisting of drivers such as "don't trust," "important men will abandon you," "you're not good enough; prove yourself!" etc. All victim, all negative (threat), and all, in Heidegger's term, "thrown."

In thinking about "thrownness," I've always visualized a potter throwing clay onto the wheel—how the clay hits the wheel sets the parameters for how the pot turns out. If someone is "thrown" to "prove yourself," they will spend their lives doing things that fit that demand, and will avoid anything that does not. It's unlikely that our friend Jim, with the twin drivers of "I'm not smart enough" and "prove myself," would be drawn to painting or music—they would not satisfy the need to appear smart—but a PhD would be just the ticket.

AWARENESS 2: COMING TO TERMS WITH THE TRAUMA

The first step in awareness is separating the facts of what happened from the interpretations, conclusions, etc., and for the person to realize that a four-year-old has been running their life. On the one hand, this "inner child" is to be appreciated, even applauded, for answering the question of survival in a way that has led to the person to succeed in life. On the other hand, it is important to realize that the strengths that led to their success have arguably also limited their development.

Richard Bach said, "Argue for your limitations, and sure enough they're yours."

But one doesn't go around arguing for their limitations, do they? Jim spent his life arguing that he was the smartest guy in the room. Think about that for a minute—Einstein is remembered for a lot of quotes, but in none of them does he ever refer to his own genius. Someone who knows they are smart doesn't have to proclaim it—only someone who is ashamed and afraid that they will be found out to be "not smart" has to advertise how smart they are. Thus, the very strategy that we set up for survival of the identity comes to be self-reinforcing; just as the person who snaps their fingers to keep tigers away, we constantly prove that our survival strategy works because we keep being traumatized and surviving.

Finally, after years of teaching others about awareness and accountability, Jim realized that it was time to take his own medicine. Working with several very skilled coaches, he first came to realize that the story of his being undervalued and disrespected and compared to Frank was just that—a story. If any of his conclusions were valid—that his parents (and everyone else) liked Frank better than they liked him, that he was the smartest person in any room he was in, that he had to prove himself—they were still only conclusions he had drawn and allowed to run his life. He looked at the facts: he, in fact, was very smart. People liked, valued, and respected him, not in spite of his (hidden) deficits, but when he was vulnerable enough to show his insecurity and fears, because of them.

Jim kept making mistakes, but then he caught himself and realized that in a meeting, two weeks earlier, he had dominated the conversation and put others down. When he had this realization, he circled back to those involved, owned his behavior, and apologized. Soon it only took a week, then days, then hours for him to become aware of having let his survival strategy run the show. And finally he found he could catch himself, before the words came out of his mouth, and remain silent. That was when he made the biggest discovery of all: when he did not dominate, didn't center himself as the main character, didn't make others feel less smart than he, people valued and appreciated what he had to say when he did speak. They listened to him!

From there on, for Jim it was all practice and a commitment to master this new way of being.

It is easy to fall into the trap of believing that, because childhood traumas occurred in the distant past, our reactions and behavior are set in stone, and there is nothing we can do about them. The fallacy in this is that while it's true that the originating event(s) occurred in the past, the experience of being triggered or re-traumatized, and surviving, is happening in the present. This is why awareness is the key first step.

RECONTEXTUALIZING THE PAST

When we become aware of the recurrence of trauma in the present, we create the possibility of creating a new context for it. The statement "context is decisive"[xxviii] has been attributed to Werner Erhard, and it points to the critical nature of both the default context and any context that may be designed in the future.

As illustrated in the Jim example, with awareness retrograde proceeds. As a person becomes aware of their triggers, the triggers gradually lose their emotional charge and become, at first, an increasingly interesting observation as they begin to lose their grip on the person. As corrective action is taken faster and faster, the person reaches a point where they become more and more reliable at stopping the reactions when they occur, or even anticipating and avoiding them. The following quote is often attributed to Viktor Frankl, author of *Man's Search for Meaning*,[xxix] particularly by Stephen Covey.[xxx]

While it's true origin is unclear, its message is critically important:

> *Between stimulus and response there is a space. In that space is our power to choose our response. In our response lies our growth and our freedom.*

"Awareness itself is curative" is another phrase with an uncertain origin; it is often attributed to Fritz Perls, the founder of Gestalt therapy.[xxxi] Why would this be so? The answer lies in the retrograde nature of awareness. When a person reaches the point where they can see and feel the emotional charge of re-traumatization and not judge it, entertain it, or have it control their actions, they create the space that Frankl refers to—a space where choice is possible.

More technically, Daniel Goleman, in *Emotional Intelligence*,[xxxii] defines the "amygdala hijack" as "an emotional response that is immediate, overwhelming, and out of measure with the actual stimulus because it has triggered a much more significant emotional threat." The key to understanding this lies in the architecture of the brain. As we saw in chapter two, the amygdala is part of what has been called "the reptilian brain," lying at the confluence of all the sensory input that comes from the rest of the central nervous system.[xxxiii]

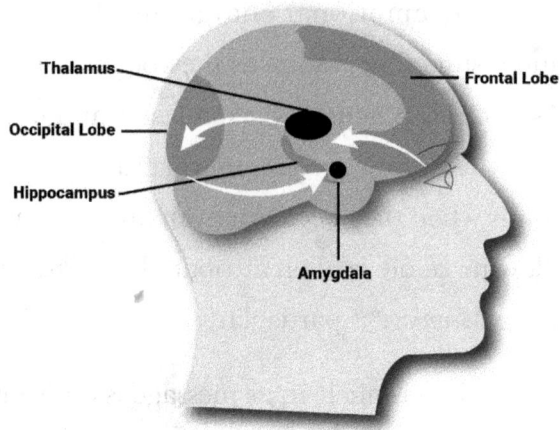

Figure 6

Before any sensory input can get to the frontal lobe (the thinking part of the brain), it must pass through the amygdala. In the "hijack," the amygdala reacts and takes over.

CHAPTER FOUR
THE ROLE LANGUAGE PLAYS

"Okay," said Jim, "I get it about the transformation triangle. I'm catching myself earlier and earlier when I get triggered, and I'm intervening to ask myself what I'm committed to in the interaction and acting accordingly. But that all seems very situational—how do I apply transformation so that the past loses its hold on me?"

His coach replied, "You ask 'who am I in the matter?'"

Jim looked confused. "What do you mean who am I? Isn't that the same as what am I committed to?"

"Not quite," his coach responded. "What you're committed to can be, as you said, situational—it could only be a way of asking what you want to have happen in the interaction. 'Who am I' is a bigger question—it goes to your purpose, vision, mission, and values."

"But how do I know the answer?" said Jim, perplexed.

"You say so."

In chapter one, we touched briefly on the importance of language. Given that we use language all the time in our everyday life, you may wonder why we are placing so much emphasis on a seemingly quotidian subject. For one thing, *how we talk is how we think*, and for the most part, we talk in the arenas of *doing* and *having*. In the normal course of our lives, we don't spend much time talking about *being*. Said another way, we use language descriptively rather than creatively. In a quote attributed to an anonymous Inuit artist:

> *Words do not label things already there. Words are like the knife of the carver: They free the idea, the thing, from the general formlessness of the outside. As a man speaks, not only is his language in a state of birth, but also the very thing about which he is talking.*

While language is extraordinarily useful for description, transformation requires acquiring skill in the creative applications of language. In this chapter, we will explore this aspect of language and the power of *committed speaking and listening*.

John Austin proposed that, along with *assertions* of facts, we use language to *do* things by using what he called "speech acts." John Searle extended the concept of Austin's speech acts and defined these in terms of two factors: "illocutionary force" and "propositional content." The latter is just what it says—the content of an utterance. The former goes to the intent of the utterance—is it a statement, a question, a command, a request, or a promise?[xxxiv] Searle's work was then expanded on by Fernando Flores.[xxxv]

Looking at current thinking on the work of Austin, Searle, Flores, and others, we can say that the following speech acts are important in modern language:

- *Declaration: To bring something into being by speaking; for example, "I pronounce you married," and "You're hired."*

- *Request: To ask that something be delivered (or an action performed) at or by a certain time.*

- *Promise: To commit that something will be delivered (or an action taken) at or by a certain time.*

- *Offer: To commit that something will be delivered (or an action taken) at or by a certain time if the respondent agrees to accept it.*

These are, in Austin's terminology, speech acts—speech that does things, as distinguished from other forms of speech such as assertions that what is being said is a fact—that it is real, evident, and demonstrable—implying a commitment to show these three qualities. For example, "The cat is on the mat," and "There was a ten foot snowfall at X ski area last weekend." Assertions may be descriptive—it's a fact that the cat is on the mat—but nothing "happens" in the world as a result of the utterance. Declarations, requests, promises, and offers, on the other hand, *create a future that would not otherwise have happened*, as in the following dialogue:

> *Jane: "Jennifer, I'd like to have lunch with you next Tuesday at the Blue Plate Diner at 12:30 p.m." (REQUEST)*
>
> *Jennifer: "I can't do it on Tuesday, but I can do it on Thursday, same time, same place." (OFFER)*
>
> *Jane: "Okay. Let's meet then." (PROMISE)*

This simple exchange, according to Austin, *does* several things. First, there is now an agreement to meet next Thursday; this appointment did not exist a moment ago. Second, a whole series of actions is launched; without the exchange, these would not have happened:

- *Both Jane and Jennifer create entries in their calendars for the lunch appointment, also blocking off travel time to and from the Blue Plate Diner.*

- *Jane calls the Blue Plate Diner and books a table.*

- *Both women check Maps to plan their route.*

- *Etc., etc.*

The point is that even as simple a transaction as this one creates a future that was not predictable before the interaction. Now take a more complex example:

> *On May 25, 1961, US President John F. Kennedy stood before Congress and proposed that the US "should commit itself to achieving the goal, before this decade is out, of landing [a human being] on the Moon and returning him safely to the Earth." This commitment, subsequently ratified by Congress, created a future that, at the time, was completely outside the realm of predictability.*
>
> *That future was fulfilled on July 20, 1969, when Astronaut Neil Armstrong and Apollo 11 Lunar Module Pilot Buzz Aldrin became the first people to land on the Moon and when, on July 24, 1969, they splashed back down safely on Earth.*

As we noted earlier, declaration is a unique speech act. As with requests, promises, and offers, declarations create a future that alters where things were headed. But unlike the other speech acts, declaration creates the future *as a context*.

Two people walk down an aisle or walk up to the desk of a justice of the peace. Those two people's relationship status, their "being" in the world, is "single." Words are said, possibly rings are exchanged, yet they remain single. Then the officiant says, "I pronounce you married," and everything changes—they're now "married." Their marriage and the promises they made become the context of their relationship until and unless some later declaration nullifies them. The same thing happens when a manager says, "You're hired," or "You're fired."

Kennedy, as President, had the authority to declare America's commitment to land a person on the Moon and bring them back safely. So a declaration that creates a new context seems to depend on the authority of the person making the declaration. The wedding officiant is authorized by the state or by a church to declare marriages. The hiring manager is authorized by their organization to hire and fire. But whence comes the authority to declare, as in Jim's case, who I am?

"I say so?" said Jim. "I don't get it."

"Yes," said the coach. "You, and only you, can answer the question 'who am I?'"

"Well, I'm a human being; I'm a son; I'm a father; I'm an American; I'm a veteran…"

"No, those are all titles that you have been given. I'm asking you, behind all that, who are you?"

"Okay, I'm caring, loving, compassionate, fearful…"

"Nope. Those are qualities you have. Let me ask you: What makes being caring, loving, and compassionate important to you?"

"They're important because I care about people."

"And what makes caring about people important to you?"

"I believe it's important because by caring about people I create a more loving and humane world."

"So who are you?"

"I am the possibility of a loving, humane world."

THE SELF CREATING ITSELF: TAKING A BOLD STAND

As in the example, with a little digging, we can get to the answer of the question. Jim's coach used what may be called the "three whys."[xxxvi]

Note that the declaration that is the reply to "who am I?" is often expressed as a possibility or life purpose. Jim is not saying he's THE possibility, as in the only one or the answer to the world's problems with humanity, but rather that he is one person, standing in for humanity where he is. Loretta Malandro[xxxvii] and Tracy Goss,[xxxviii] among others have referred to this as "taking a bold stand."

But the question remains, where does the authority to declare oneself or take a bold stand come from?

"Great! But where do you get the authority to declare that?"

"Oh, I guess I don't have the authority, do I?"

"Not so fast. Who says you are the possibility of a loving, humane world?"

"Well, I do, I guess."

"And who said you could say that?"

"I did."

"Then where does the authority lie?"

"With me. I can declare my own life."

"So you declare you can declare?"

"Yes, I guess so. Yes...I authorize myself."

Bear with me here—if this is the first time you have encountered this idea, it can be tough sledding, and it can't be made much easier without destroying the beauty of it. It requires something we don't usually do in language, and that is self-reflexive or self-referential thinking. For example, take the following statement: *This statement is false.* The statement is self-referential in that it literally refers to itself. It is also a paradox, since if it is true, then it is false, and vice versa. This is why self-referential statements are often mind-bending.

In the case of human beings, consider the following from Kierkegaard's 18 essay "The Sickness unto Death":[xxxix]

> *[A human being] is spirit. But what is spirit? Spirit is the self. But what is the self?* **The self is a relation that relates itself to its own self.**... *The self is not the relation but (consists in the fact) that the relation relates itself to its own self.... [A human being] is a synthesis of the infinite and the finite, of the temporal and the eternal, of freedom and necessity; in short, it is a synthesis. A synthesis*

is a relation between two factors. So regarded, [a human being] is not yet a self.

In the relation between two, the relation is the third term as a negative unity, and the two relate themselves to the relation, and in the relation to the relation; such a relation is that between soul and body when [a human being] is regarded as soul. If on the contrary the relation relates itself to its own self, the relation is then the positive third term, and this is the self.

Such a relation, which relates itself to its own self (that is to say, a self), must either have constituted itself or have been constituted by another.

* * *

Such a derived, constituted relation is the human self, a relation which relates itself to its own self, and in relating itself to its own self, relates itself to another.... This formula (i.e., that the self is constituted by another) is the expression for the total dependence of the relation (the self, namely), the expression for the fact that the self cannot of itself attain and remain in equilibrium and rest by itself, but only by relating itself to that power which constituted the whole relation.

Indeed, so far is it from being true that this second form of despair (despair at willing to be one's own self) denotes only a particular kind of despair, that on the contrary all despair can in the last analysis be reduced to this....

This then is the formula which describes the condition of the self when despair is

completely eradicated: by relating itself to its own self and by willing to be itself, the self is grounded transparently in the power which posited it.

The despair that Kierkegaard refers to is the feeling that accompanies looking to some power outside ourselves for the answer to the question "Who am I?" And as he points out in the last paragraph quoted, that despair is "eradicated" when a person relates to themselves as the "power which posited it"—that is, the self declaring itself.

When a person comes to the realization that they have the power to constitute themselves beyond how their life experiences of trauma have constituted them, they move to that power to choose that Frankl refers to. **Now there is a choice—the default context of their survival strategy or a context of their own design. In that context of empowerment, the world shows up differently—***if I am the one who has designed my life, and if past shadows of "I'm not good enough, smart enough, etc." are now seen as myths created under duress, then blame is pointless and victimhood is an illusion. This is personal transformation.*

"I created a vision of David in my mind and simply carved away everything that was not David."[xl] That quote may be apocryphal, but it has long been attributed to Michelangelo, and it describes beautifully the process that follows the initial declaration of transformation. First, the possibility is created by declaration, and then the person goes to work putting it into practice and making the possibility a reality.

It is this last piece that is the rub. To come to terms with one's past traumas, the survival strategy that was built in answer to Berne's question, and the life that was created in the space left over after having given up on the possibility of anything beyond the strategy—being resigned to living within those limits—is hard enough. **To give up blaming oneself, others, and the circumstances and declare a new possibility is both liberating and daunting.**

In the next chapter, we will examine what it takes to translate transformation from declaration into living or, as Heidegger put it, from "being into being-in-the-world."

CHAPTER FIVE

SUSTAINING TRANSFORMATION: ACCOUNTABILITY, RESPONSIBILITY, AND AUTHENTICITY

M artin Heidegger wrote extensively about what he called the "being of human beings." Heidegger used the term "*Dasein*," usually translated as existence, but by which Heidegger meant the distinct kind of entity that human beings are, specifically that, for human beings, being is an issue (a concept similar to Kierkegaard's "self creating itself"). According to Stephen Mulhall in *The Routledge Guidebook to Heidegger's Being and Time*, "while inanimate objects merely persist through time and plants and nonhuman animals have their lives determined entirely by the demands of survival and reproduction, human beings *lead their lives*."[xli]

Another of Heidegger's key ideas is that there is "no being without being-in-the-world." Said in more familiar terms, being functions as a context for the "in-the-world" activities of doing and having.

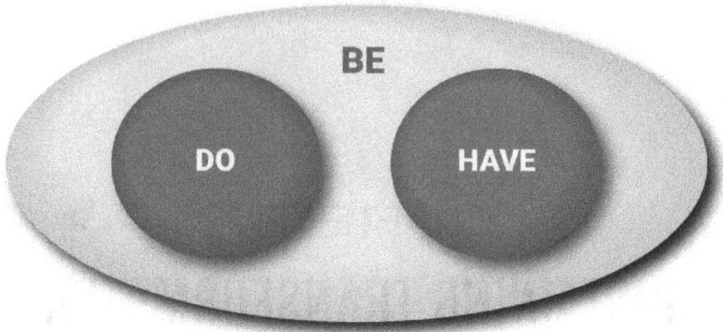

Figure 7

Heidegger distinguishes this contextual meaning of being (Dasein) as follows: The lowercase "**being**" is, for our purposes, what we have heretofore referred to as identity or ego. The uppercase "**Being**" is that which is realized when the self creates itself by declaration.

In language, as we've seen, Being is created by declaration as I self-authorize by saying who I am. It serves the same function as replying to the childhood question that Berne phrased as "What do I have to do to survive around here?" It is worth noting that the childhood question is one of *doing* and *having* (survival)—absent the capacity for abstract thinking, the young child hasn't the capacity to consider issues of being.

Often, declaration of self takes the form of a vision or purpose—a reason for being (though Being, which is declared *ex nihilo*, or out of nothing, needs no reason); this brings Being into the world as a context for action.

When action is added to vision, it becomes a mission, which gives a direction to action. For example, the declaration of purpose might be "I will create a world in which everyone is treated fairly and justly." The declarer might then consider how they might best fulfill that purpose, and then further declare that they will do this through engaging in social activism. So they have, in effect, declared a mission—"I will create a world in which everyone is treated justly *by engaging and speaking out wherever I see injustice.*" **It is important to note here that the vision and mission are aspirational—they are not achievable as goals, but they provide a context for viewing self, others, and the world.**

When the person has committed to the vision and mission, values naturally emerge. A person with this vision of fairness and justice, for example, might have strong values of compassion and fairness. Values, in turn, translate into practices such as kindness, assuming positive intent, and others. These can vary widely. If we imagine two people, each with a vision of justice and a mission of activism, it is possible for one to have a value of nonviolence and the other to have a value of fighting for justice.

None of this should be understood as absolute. It is tempting to view transformation as a road-to-Damascus conversion in which, suddenly, a person becomes someone completely different from who they were. Existentially, this is the case—the context for the person's life has changed, and they now view their existence as their own creation, rather than a struggle to survive against enemies who are no longer a threat. On the other hand, to quote Erhard:

> *Transformation is not an event. It doesn't have the properties of things or experiences. It has no position, no location in time, no beginning, no middle, and no end. It doesn't look like anything or feel like anything. You could say it's a shift in the basis of experience from self as point of view or from self as direct experience to self as self, or self as simply being.*

> *True transformation is the recovery by the self of the generating principles with which self creates the self. Transformation is self as self—the space in which being occurs, or to put it another way, it is the being of abstraction or the context which the being of abstraction is.*[xlii]

Once again, we find ourselves in the slippery territory of self-reflective statements. Think of it this way: **until one engages with self-transformation, the conclusions and interpretations about self, others, and the world that form the survival strategy function as the default context that determines how the world shows up**.

In Jim's example, events in his life showed up as "proof" that he was not smart enough and that he had to prove himself. When Jim declared, first, his authority to declare, and, second, his desire to create a loving, humane world, he reconstituted himself and created a new context for the world to show up in. The declaration "I have the power to declare" (sometimes rendered as "I am my word") is the self creating itself.

The initial commitment is a crucial step. Consider this well-known quote from W. H. Murray:

> *Until one is committed, there is always hesitancy, the chance to draw back, always ineffectiveness.*
>
> *Concerning all acts of initiative and creation, there is one elementary truth, the ignorance of which kills countless ideas and splendid plans.*
>
> *The moment one commits oneself, then providence moves too.*

Multitudes of things occur to help that which otherwise could never be. A stream of events issues from the decision, raising to one's favor all manner of unforeseen accidents, meetings, and material assistance, which no one could have dreamed would come his way.

I have learned deep respect for one of Goethe's couplets: "**Whatever you can do or dream you can, begin it. Boldness has genius, power, and magic in it.**"[xliii]

Once the new context is committed to, then the real work begins—the work of practice, over time, in community[xliv] I am grateful to my colleague Rayona Sharpnack for this formulation, which I learned from her years ago and have used ever since:

Practice

- *Applying the new context through keeping the vision, mission, and values in the forefront of awareness.*

- *Catching and cleaning up mistakes—abandoning behaviors that are inconsistent with the new context.* **Transformation is an art of correction, not perfection.**

Over Time

- *Given the unfamiliarity of the behaviors associated with the new context and the tenaciousness of the ego's drive to survive and to reinstate the default context, practice is essential and must be carried on in the face of frustration and failure.*

In Community

- *This aspect is crucial. While enlightenment may come to hermits sitting in a cave, the purpose of transformation is to alter the quality of the person's life and, by extension, the lives of those with whom they come into contact. This requires:*

- *That the commitment to the new context be public.*

- *That the person, in addition to holding themselves accountable for the new vision, mission, and values, be willing to be held accountable by others as well.*

In a very real sense the person has spent their entire life training those around them to believe that they "are" a certain way, the way the survival strategy requires them to be. Those with whom they associate have learned how to interact with that persona, and will continue to do so until they learn to interact in a different way. Through the triple discipline—practice, over time, and in community—the transformed individual will "retrain" their environment to their new way of being.

"All right," said Jim, "I've declared that I have the power to declare, and that I am the possibility of a loving, humane world. I'm making it my mission to bring more humane practices to the companies and executives I work with by introducing new practices and ways of being to them, and I am committed to values of compassion, integrity, kindness, and justice. There's just one problem."

"What's that?" said the coach.

"When I say all that, it feels right and genuine, but when I go out and act on it in the world, it doesn't feel like me—it's not who I am."

"Well, it's who you are if you say it's who you are, but I think what you mean is that it's not a way of being that you're used to."

"Exactly," Jim said. "It feels put on or phony, and I don't think anyone is going to take me seriously."

"Well," the coach said, "it will definitely feel that way for a while, and you will catch yourself falling into your old patterns. But if you don't keep at it, you're not likely to succeed."

"But how?"

"I'd start by looking at where in your life your way of being has had a negative impact on people around you and where you have felt like a victim. Start there to clean things up."

SUSTAINING THE TRANSFORMATION 1: CLEANUPS AND FORGIVENESS

In my experience of coaching a great many people over the past decades, I have never run into a default context or survival strategy that was entirely benign. To be sure, most of the time, there are benign, even beneficial, aspects. For example, people whose childhood experiences left them withdrawn and self-involved (narcissistic personalities) may come up with brilliant inventions to show the world they don't need anyone else. People who live under constant imagined threats (paranoid personalities) may become highly successful in law enforcement. The list goes on. Pretty much, all survival strategies have redeeming qualities, and what I believe is the basic goodness of human beings manages, somehow, to shine through.

However, the root of any survival strategy lies, first, in threat and trauma; therefore, damage to others, intended or not, is inevitable, and feelings of hurt and victimization as well. In relationships, the impact of the survival strategies manifest in two categories of wounds: resentment and regret.

- **Resentment:** *Feelings of anger, hurt, etc. associated with something someone did or did not do to me.*

- **Regret:** *Feelings of remorse, shame, guilt, etc. associated with something I believe I did or did not do to someone else.*

These feelings may be strong or weak, but they persist and are kept secret. I suggest to people I coach that they think about a scale from minus ten to positive ten and map the people in their life onto that scale in terms of affinity—zero would be neutral; positive ten, a strong liking or sympathy for; and negative ten, antipathy or extreme dislike. In the case of anyone below zero—even if it's by only one-tenth—look for resentment or regret.

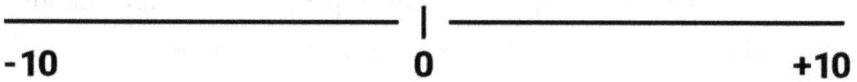

-10   **0**   **+10**

Figure 8

Once you've found the cause, then there is cleanup to do. This can take many forms:

- **Apology**—*Offer an apology for holding on to the resentment or regret and allowing it to interfere with the relationship, whether working or personal.*

- **Forgiveness**—*Declare the matter forgiven and reset the relationship to before the occurrence, or ask the person to forgive the offense. (To forgive is to give up the desire or power to punish.)*

- **Promise**—*Make a promise about how you will handle offenses in the future.*

- **Declaration**—*Declare your commitment to the relationship, cooperation, friendship, or whatever is authentic, even indifference, but give up your resentment or regret.*

The practice of cleaning up residual feelings from lapses in the past or present, as quickly as possible, will go a long way toward retraining your environment as to whom you are committed to being and enlisting allies in your transformational journey.

SUSTAINING THE TRANSFORMATION 2: RESPONSIBILITY

The importance of cleanups cannot be overstated; they highlight the key to the sustainability of any personal transformation—taking responsibility.

> *All it takes to make a difference is the courage to stop proving I was right in being unable to make a difference…to stop assigning cause for my inability to the circumstances outside*

myself and to be willing to have been that way, and to see
that the fear of being a failure is a lot less important than the
unique opportunity I have to make a difference.

"To be willing to have been that way" is key to this quote. Said in terms of the transformation triangle, "to own how you have been being," declare or re-declare your commitment to a new way of being, and take action in line with that commitment. As we've noted, this means giving up blame, being right about how you were treated (forgiving), and releasing shame. This last is critical—it amounts to forgiving yourself for the restrictions you created in service of what appeared to be necessary to survive.

SUSTAINING THE TRANSFORMATION 3: ACCOUNTABILITY

Accountability is key to sustaining transformation and having it alter the course of one's life. The context of the transformation triangle precludes shame, blame, and refuge in the circumstances ("I was late because of the traffic."). Accountability says in effect, "If it happened in my world, I am responsible."

The key principles of accountability are:[xlvi]

- **Accountability is based on a promise.** *Being accountable means you agree to identify yourself as the sole agent for an outcome,* *regardless of the unpredictability of what may happen between the time you make the promise and the time you commit to fulfilling it.*

- **Accountability means activities aren't enough.** *You've promised an outcome, and if you don't deliver that outcome, it won't matter how hard you tried or how much you wanted to.*

- **Accountability is neither shared nor conditional.** *Accountability is without condition. If it's your promise, you are accountable, regardless of circumstances. Individuals must go beyond traditional reasonableness and use any ethical means to produce the result.*

- **Accountability is meaningless without positive consequences.** *Accountability is not about finding fault, assigning blame, or meting out punishments. It is about achieving success and learning from mistakes.*

Referring back to the discussion of speech acts, it is critical to understand that promises are not transactional. In other words, a promise is not something I hand over to you with no accountability on your part. A transactional promise is a setup for blame. Blame and shame are incompatible with accountability.

Rather, a promise creates a *relationship of commitment*—a relationship in which both parties are held to the promise, and the promisor (the one making the promise) agrees *to identify themself as the sole agent for an outcome.* In such a relationship, it is the job of the promisee (the one accepting the promise) to do their due diligence to be sure that the promisor understands what is required to deliver on the promise and either has the wherewithal to deliver the results or has the support to acquire what is needed along the way. The promisee may also set milestones to check on progress and otherwise take responsibility (though not accountability) for the results being delivered.

The path of personal transformation is not easy. Robert S. de Ropp (1913–1987) was an English biochemist who, after retiring from biochemistry, became a writer in the fields of human potential and the search for spiritual realization. In the latter realm, one of his most influential books is *The Master Game*, in which he says the following (what he calls "the Master Game" is equivalent to what we are calling personal transformation):

> *Seek, above all, for a game worth playing. Such is the advice of the oracle to modern [people]. Having found the game, play it with intensity—play as if your life and sanity depend on it. (They do depend on it.) Follow the example of the French existentialists and flourish a banner bearing the word "engagement."*

> *Though nothing means anything and all roads are marked "No Exit," yet move as if your movements had some purpose. If life does not seem to offer a game worth playing, then invent one. For it must be clear, even to the most clouded intelligence, that any game is better than no game.*

> *But although it is safe to play the Master Game, this has not served to make it popular. It still remains the most demanding and difficult of games, and in our society, there are few who play. Contemporary [people], hypnotized by the glitter of…gadgets, [have] little contact with [their] inner world, concerns [themselves] with outer, not inner, space. But the Master Game is played entirely in the inner world, a vast and complex territory about which [people] know very little. The aim of the game is true awakening, full development of the powers latent in man.*

The game can be played only by people whose observations of themselves and others have led them to a certain conclusion; namely, that [a human's] ordinary state of consciousness, [their] so-called waking state, is not the highest level of consciousness of which [they are] capable. In fact, this state is so far from real awakening that it could appropriately be called a form of somnambulism, a condition of "waking sleep."

Once a person has reached this conclusion, [they are] no longer able to sleep comfortably. A new appetite develops within [them], the hunger for real awakening, for full consciousness. [One] realizes that [one] sees, hears, and knows only a tiny fraction of what [one] could see, hear, and know, that [they live] in the poorest, shabbiest of rooms in [their] inner dwelling, and that [they] could enter other rooms, beautiful and filled with treasures, the windows of which look out on eternity and infinity.

The solitary player lives today in a culture that is more or less totally opposed to the aims [they have] set [themselves], that does not recognize the existence of the Master Game, and [that] regards players of this game as queer or slightly mad. The player thus confronts great oppositions from the culture in which [they live] and must strive with forces, which tend to bring [their] game to a halt before it has even started. Only by finding a teacher and becoming part of the group of pupils that that teacher has collected about [them] can the player find encouragement and support. Otherwise [they] simply forget [their] aim, or wander off down some side road and lose [themselves].

Here it is sufficient to say that the Master Game can never be made easy to play. It demands all that a [person] has, all [their] feelings, all [their] thoughts, all [their] resources—physical and spiritual. If [they try]to play it in a half-hearted way or [try] to get results by unlawful means, [they] run the risk of destroying [their] own potential. For this reason, it is better not to embark on the game at all than to play it half-heartedly. [xlvii]

To close the personal transformation section and our story of Jim, here is one last quote, this one from the poet e.e. cummings. In it, cummings is responding to a young person who wrote asking cummings how to become a poet. He might easily have been responding to Jim about transformation:

A poet is somebody who is being, and who expresses his or her being through words. This may sound easy. It isn't.

A lot of people think or believe or know they are being, but that's thinking or believing or knowing, not being, and poetry is being, not knowing or believing or thinking.

Almost anybody can learn to think or believe or know, but not a single human being can be taught to be. Why? Because whenever you think or you believe or you know, you are a lot of other people, but the moment you are being, you're nobody-but-yourself.

To be nobody-but-yourself in a world which is doing its best, night and day, to make you everybody-else, means to fight the hardest battle which any human being can fight, and never stop fighting.

As for expressing nobody-but-yourself in words, that means working just a little harder than anybody who isn't a poet can possibly imagine. Why? Because nothing is quite as easy as using words like somebody else. We all of us do exactly this nearly all of the time, and whenever we do it, we are not poets.

If, at the end of your first ten or fifteen years of fighting and working and being, you find you've written one line of one poem, you'll be very lucky indeed.

And so my advice to all young people who wish to become poets is: Do something easy, like learning to blow up the world, unless you're not only willing, but glad, to be and work and fight till you die.

Does this sound dismal? It isn't. It's the most wonderful life on earth, or so I feel. [xlviii]

CHAPTER SIX

ORGANIZATIONAL TRANSFORMATION: HOW WE GOT WHERE WE ARE

In the first chapter of this book, we defined transformation *as a shift in the locus of identity from content to context*. It is this definition that justifies using the term "transformation" for both individuals and organizations.

As with individuals, organizations have an identity often called a brand. As we will see, organizations also have *being* (culture), *doing* (process), and *having* (results). As with individuals, organizations have a default culture and the possibility of designing a culture that transcends the default.

THE DEFAULT CULTURE OF ORGANIZATION

What we know as an organization today has evolved from ancient tribal civilizations through militaries (most notably the Roman military), the Catholic Church, feudalism, colonialism, and the Industrial Revolution. The thread that runs through all of these is *hierarchy.*

For much of the 300,000 years or so that modern humans (Homo sapiens) have existed, there exists little or no evidence of hierarchy. Humans lived in small bands of hunter-gatherers consisting of a few dozen people at most, and there was little formal leadership or structure. Any attempt to dominate the group was collectively suppressed—bands were self-organizing, effortlessly collaborative, and small enough that everyone had a personal relationship with everyone else. Trust was high, and people looked out for one another. While conflict did still occur, on the whole, these were highly effective societies, and the human brain has perfectly evolved for this kind of existence.

Around 10,000 years ago, with the advent of agriculture, small farming villages of a few hundred people each started to emerge. As people filled the land, villages came into conflict with each other. More than anything else, conflict created the need to organize centrally, and hierarchy arose as the ability to organize and coordinate soldiers greatly improved their effectiveness. A properly led army with a good strategy could easily defeat more skilled warriors who fought individually or in small bands. They proved more effective in battle than those with no formal organization, strategy, or training. In the age of warfare, more hierarchical societies outcompeted less centralized ones overall.

The first centralized societies began to emerge 7,500 years ago in Mesopotamia as simple chiefdoms composed of a few thousand people. Personal connections and high levels of cooperation and trust faded in importance, in favor of rules administered by force. As warfare became increasingly important, weapons production and standing armies started to emerge, all supported by hierarchy.

Over the past 10,0000 years, humans have moved from small foraging bands to centralized nation-states consisting of hundreds of millions of people. From the Catholic Church to the Roman Empire to Max Weber's twentieth-century bureaucratic management structure, we are now living in a system in which the hierarchical pyramid is seen as the only option. This is the default context or paradigm. How else could large numbers of people possibly be mobilized to pull together toward a common goal?

The unquestioned use of centralized hierarchies in organizations reached a high in the late nineteenth and early twentieth centuries. The inventions of electricity, internal combustion engine, and telephone transformed energy, transportation, and communications, respectively, and enabled the growth of larger organizations than had ever been seen before. Hierarchies worked well during this time of relative stability, a time when efficiently exploiting existing business models was the path to great commercial success.

In 1910, Frederick Winslow Taylor published *The Principles of Scientific Management*,[xlix] in which he espoused four principles:

- *Science, not rule of thumb*

- *Harmony, not discord*

- *Cooperation, not individualism*

- *Maximum output, not restricted output*

Taylor was of the view that implementation of these principles required hierarchical supervision to ensure adherence to the system:

> *In the past the man has been first; in the future the system must be first. This in no sense, however, implies that great men are not needed. On the contrary, the first object of any*

good system must be that of developing first-class men; and under systematic management, the best man rises to the top more certainly and more rapidly than ever before.[l]

Taylor was also of the view that workers did not want to work, and so hierarchical supervision was necessary:

Hardly a competent workman can be found who does not devote a considerable amount of time to studying just how slowly he can work and still convince his employer that he is going at a good pace.[li]

Taylor's work crystallized the default context for organizations—their purpose was output (later summarized by economist Milton Friedman as the "Profit Doctrine,"[lii] more commonly known as "the Friedman Doctrine"). This doctrine holds that the social responsibility of business is to increase its profits or shareholder value. Taylor, not coincidentally, was the originator of "time/motion," or efficiency, studies.

Today, however, the world is a different place. High levels of volatility, uncertainty, complexity, and ambiguity mean that organizations must now structure themselves for agility, not efficiency, embracing innovation and the continual reinvention of their products, services, and business models. Increasingly, hierarchy is giving way to the forms of organizational structure that emphasize interconnectedness and collaboration. This builds on our evolutionary past as a self-organizing, collaborative species that thrives on connection and emergent leadership, rather than on the efforts of an army of formal managers.[liii]

It seems we do our best creative-knowledge work as autonomous, cross-functional, high-trust teams working toward a common vision. Teams can easily collaborate with other teams, customers, and leaders as part of a wider network structure—a team of teams, if you will. This approach leads to teams that are more creative and more adaptive. These types of teams are better suited to both our ancestral past and the fast-paced, complex business climate of the twenty-first century.

Despite the changing environment, there have been many efforts over the past hundred years to change the *process* of organizations without changing the *context*, even though the importance of context has long been recognized. For example, Peter Drucker, probably the leading management thinker of the twentieth century, is widely quoted to have said "culture eats strategy for breakfast." Notwithstanding that, efforts such as total quality management (TQM), Kaizen, and business process reengineering (BPR) have continued to emerge and, as we will see, fail.

If total quality management was the management "answer" of the late 1980s, business process reengineering took its place in the first half of the '90s. *Fortune*, in its August 23, 1993, issue,[liv] proclaimed reengineering "the hot new managing tool," this despite citing an alarming failure rate of reengineering projects and noting that, even when reengineering succeeds, it is "almost always accompanied by pain—or at least some unpleasant side effects, such as causing executives' hair to fall out."

According to *Fortune*, management consulting firms large and small were flocking to reengineering as the new weapon of choice in the competitive wars. Despite the consulting firms' claims to have quintupled their business in five years of reengineering consulting, a 1991 survey by Index found that one-quarter of nearly 300 North American companies involved in reengineering reported that they were not meeting their goals. In an article in *Insights Quarterly,*

Michael Hammer, literally the author of the book on reengineering (along with CSC Index CEO James Champy), stated his belief that the failure rate of reengineering is much higher—**"on the order of 70%."** Hammer and others attribute this failure rate to resistance to change, lack of understanding of what was really involved, or lack of nerve on the part of client companies. Such explanations are suspect, preserving as they do the validity of the model while placing the blame for the failures on the clients.

Another possibility for the failure of reengineering is that it is an attempt to change the process while leaving the context intact. Context, which we have noted is decisive at the personal level, is no less so for organizations. For individuals, the context, called identity, is the survival strategy; for organizations, it is the default culture.

We can summarize the default culture of organizations as follows:

- *Hierarchical*—*There is a chain of command, and it is adhered to. There is a back-channel network that subverts the chain of command.*

- *Information*—*Information is currency, and it is banked and hoarded rather than freely shared. There is sub-rosa trafficking in information.*

- *Blame*—*Responsibility is considered, at best, a fifty-fifty proposition. "I did my job, so if it failed; it must be someone else who didn't do theirs." This culture has been described as a cycle of* **enthusiasm, disillusionment, panic, search for the guilty, punishment of the innocent, rewards for the uninvolved.**[lv]

DESIGNING A NEW CULTURE OF ORGANIZATION

As with individuals, organizations have the capability of designing a culture that is more effective than the default culture. Earlier, we defined transformation as a shift in the locus of identity from content to context. For an organization, this means shifting from being acted upon by outside forces (market, economy, customer capriciousness, disruptive technologies) to being defined by the space in which their market or industry occurs.

Often this is accomplished by inventing a new technology or process. In 1964, Xerox Corporation introduced and patented the first commercial fax machine.[lvi] Prior to that time, transmission of documents by physical delivery was the accepted and only option. Xerox's invention and subsequent improvements positioned the company as the creator of the market, much as they did with the copy machine, making Xerox, for a time, the eponym for copying.

But invention is not the only way for an organization to transform. What personal and organizational transformations have in common is that they are both accomplished by declaration of a new way of being, followed by putting that way of being into practice. A person or a group of people take on shifting an organization from the default culture in which individuals are subject to the pressures of the culture ("the way things are done around here") to a new declared culture.

As with personal transformation, the general rubric of organizational transformation has four steps:

First: Examination of the organization's default context and how it is working in today's environment.

We have always depended on new business through referrals—that's how the organization started—and it's no longer working. This has made us subject to forces over which we have no control as our only source of business development.

Second: Recognition of what the default context has cost the organization in productivity, ROE, employee turnover, and engagements, etc.

> *This dependence on referrals has forced us to compromise our standards and has limited our public perception as we often have to fly under others' banners. It has meant that revenues are up and down and unreliable, and we have had trouble keeping clients and personnel.*

Third: Creation of and commitment to a new and more desirable culture, and the translation of this into new organizational vision, mission, and values.

> *We are a unique stand-alone brand that brings outstanding value to our clients by showing them how to transform their organizational culture into one that is more equitable, productive, and vibrant. We do this through our values of integrity, respect, collaboration, and valuing each individual's unique contribution.*

Fourth: Commitment to a created body of cultural practices that are consistent with the new culture and displace the old practices that are unproductive or inconsistent with the values.

> *We have adopted cultural practices that reflect this culture and encourage our clients to do the same.*

While each organization will design its culture consistent with its industry and the larger culture in which it operates, in all of the companies we have worked with across a wide range of industries, we find that the designed cultures have the following characteristics in common:

- *Accountability*

- *Integrity*

- *Complete, open, honest communication*

- *Committed partnership*

ACCOUNTABILITY

A culture of accountability is one that is based on the results that the individual, team, department, or entire organization promises to produce. A promise will have one of two outcomes. In the best case, the promised results will be achieved or exceeded. In the worst case, what is achieved will be less than (or later than) what was promised, and lessons will be learned that will improve performance in the future.

Thus, the key to a culture of accountability is the setting of and committing to results to be produced. The *process* of accountability then becomes a matter of first acknowledging the outcomes and then assessing what worked well, what could be improved, and what could be changed.

A few things are critical to consider here. In a culture of account-ability, accountability is 100-0, not 50-50.[lvii] That is, my delivering what I promised does not depend on you or on the circumstances.

My colleague Dr. Loretta Malandro has written and taught exten-sively on this subject, and in her book *Fearless Leadership*, she relates that in Ancient Rome, when an arch was built and the scaffolding ready to be removed, the lead engineer of the arch was required to stand under it. She points out that if the arch were to fail, he would be there to be accountable.[lviii]

For 100-0 accountability, the distinction between the world of *blame* (persecutor-rescuer-victim) and that of *accountability* is crucial, particularly as regards blaming the circumstances. Valuable learning is highly unlikely if blame is in the equation, as it will always be easier to blame oneself (victim/guilt), others (victim/persecutor), or the circumstances (victim/powerless) than to examine what was done that didn't work well, what was not done, etc.

Both the promisor and the promisee need to be cognizant that there are different levels of promises. In the world of blame, promises are made to avoid conflict or are based on good intentions. In the latter case, the promisor will blame the promisee (fear of saying no, imbalance of power), and in the former, circumstances will be seen to have intervened ("stuff happens"). In the world of accountability, promises are made with a clear view of realities and resources (resources at hand and resources that are needed), or perhaps with a level of commitment that will succeed in spite of circumstances.

Before a promise is finalized, there must be clear understanding on both people's part of the degree to which the promise is malleable and the process for making changes, as well as the circumstances (if any) under which the promise can be revoked and the consequences for doing so.

If there is no clear promise (a specific delivery address or time), any conversation about accountability will be a pretense. For example, if a group doesn't have a clear set of agreements about attendance, punctuality, communication, etc., then no one is accountable for being there, being there on time, notifying others they won't be there, etc.—accountability is impossible.

No one can *make* another person accountable. For a promise to be valid, it must be a voluntary act. Some things are based on implicit promises—for example, when I accept a driver's license, the state considers me to have promised to obey traffic laws, and it will hold me accountable if I don't. In a culture of accountability, the implicit promises are:

> *I will hold myself to account, I will offer others support in*
> *holding themselves to account (support accountability), and*
> *I will be willing to be supported by others (called to account).*

The final act of accountability is "closing the loop"—acknowledging that the promise was kept or reporting that it wasn't (rather than waiting to be called on it or hoping no one will notice). A promise sets up an expectation, and the failure to fulfill on a promise will likely have an impact on the other person, at the very least disappointment and possibly the inability of the promisee to keep other promises he has made based on the promise made to him. So accountability includes being accountable for the impact of revoking, changing, or not keeping a promise. It's called "cleaning it up," and it goes a long way toward restoring trust and confidence in the relationship.

INTEGRITY

The term "integrity" can have many meanings, including some that, as Michael Jensen points out, are "in the arenas of morality, ethics, and legality."[lix] As Jensen did, we want to take integrity out of these arenas and into a more neutral account. In 1974, the Institute for Cultural Affairs founded the first of what would become a group of training schools for human development in Maliwada, India. That school published a statement titled "On Integrity" that captures what integrity is for our purposes (updated for pronouns):

> We are going to visit the arena of Profound Humanness called "integrity." Sometimes "integrity" is reduced to mean a kind of moral uprightness and steadfastness, in the sense of saying, "She has too much integrity to ever take a bribe."
>
> But profound integrity goes far beyond this. Sometimes, in order to distinguish it from the more limited popular usage, it is called "secondary integrity." This is the integrity which is not constrained by limited moralities, however well-intentioned. The integrity that is profound living is the singularity of thrust of a life committed and ordering every dimension of the self towards that commitment. Thus the self is in fact shaped by the self and focused towards that commitment. You can say that an audacious creation of the self takes place in integrity, without which you are simply the creation of the various forces impacting you in your society.
>
> Thus, the basis of integrity is a destinal resolve—a resolve that chooses and sets your destiny and out of which your whole life is ordered. The object of that resolve is the ultimate decision of each person, and each person makes that choice, consciously or unconsciously. To do so with awareness is the height of one's responsibility. It is incarnate freedom. It is what real freedom looks like. When a person has thus exercised their freedom, they realize that to be true to themself ever thereafter, they have a unique position to look at

the values of society. They are no longer bound by the opinions and codes of others but reevaluates them on the basis of their impact on the destinal resolve.

Thus, the person of integrity is continuously engaged in a societal transvaluation, a moving across the values of society and reinterpreting them in line with life's thrust. It does not give the liberty of ignoring his society, but one's obligation transcends the conformity of living within the codes and mores of his society. Thus the person of profound integrity always seems to not quite fit with their fellows, but their actions are always appropriate for them, even to those who oppose them.

No matter how odd the person of profound integrity appears to their neighbors, they experience themself as securely anchored. While they are clear that this world is not their home, nevertheless they experience themself as having found their native vale. They experience an eternal at-one-ness, not so much with the currents and waves of activity around them, but with the deeper trends of history itself. Amid the flux of wavering to and from that is so evident in others, they experience an inexplicable rootedness, as though having sunk a taproot deep into the foundation of the earth itself. Though they experience life as a long journey, even an endless journey, towards the object of their resolve, yet they never sense themself as a stranger on the journey. It's as if they'd been there before. Original integrity is experienced primarily by this sense of at-one-ness [sic].

Kierkegaard once wrote a book about this kind of integrity that he titled, Purity of Heart Is to Will One Thing. *An ancient philosopher focused his wisdom around this integrity with the advice, "Know yourself, and to your own self, be true."*

In short, then, by "integrity," we mean declaring who you are and acting consistent with that declaration. This is true at all levels of transformation—personal and organizational.

COMPLETE, OPEN, HONEST COMMUNICATION

My friend and colleague Craig Clark summarized this principle:

Speak honestly and clearly in a way that moves the action forward. Say what you mean. Ask questions for clarity, share ideas, and be willing to raise issues, even if they may create conflict, when it is needed for success or maintaining collaboration. Address issues directly with those who are involved or affected. Take responsibility for getting your message across.

How many times over the years have I kept quiet or candy-coated a communication out of a concern that I would anger someone, lose a relationship with someone or look foolish? Too many to count. In a recent conversation with a client, I suggested that most breakdowns, if not all, are the result of some conversation that was not had. Too many times over the years I would look back and realize the opportunity I had missed to contribute genuine value to moving the game forward. Further, It took a long time for me to learn that every time I didn't speak up, whatever I didn't speak up about, got buried and slowly started to grow until at some point I had built a case against an individual, a group, or an organization. Meanwhile building doubt about myself. Opportunities were missed and resentments were nurtured.

A big part of the problem was me confusing "straight talk" with being abrasive, confrontational, or righteous. I had a limiting belief that I could either be straight about something or I could be respectful. Learning to put these two together is a powerful discovery. What follows is this: There is very little one cannot say, no matter how contentious, if the communication is delivered with respect. It takes respecting oneself enough to call out the issue that may have kept the game from moving forward. It takes respecting others enough and being big enough to be able to speak straight, respectfully, even if it's not good news. Straight talk has power, efficiency, and simplicity when it is grounded in respect.[lx]

COMMITTED PARTNERSHIP

"Committed partnership" is a principle proposed by Loretta Malandro.[lxi] In my work with Dr. Malandro and her firm, working with organizations around the world, I can say that it is probably the most powerful principle in establishing and sustaining transformation in organizations.

Committed partnership builds on the other principles of accountability, integrity, and communication. Fundamentally, it means each person in an organization committing to the success of each other person and to fulfilling the organization's vision and mission. Committed partnership is a set of declarations and promises made by one person to another. An example is:

- *We stand for the success of each other, both publicly and privately.*

- *We honor and fulfill commitments.*

- *We talk straight, responsibly.*

- *We align emotionally and intellectually.*

- *We hold each other accountable.*[lxii]

If you had any doubt that, in this work of organizational transformation, we had left the realm of business as usual, this should put that doubt to rest. In the world of organization, commitments such as these are extremely rare. As Malandro points out, they require a high degree of trust, giving up the "right" to talk about others in a negative way, giving up blame, withholding information, and they go a long way toward breaking down hierarchy and substituting partnership and accountability for command and control.

As anyone who has been in a committed partnership will attest, it is an extraordinary relationship. First of all, the trust involved is unconditional or, as Malandro terms it, "granted rather than earned." For most of us, trust is viewed as if it were a bank account that grows with deposits (meeting expectations) and diminishes with withdrawals (broken promises and unmet expectations). With unconditional trust—trust is a context; within that context, failures do not diminish the trust, but offer opportunities to reinforce both the trust and the relationship.

The commitments to *stand for your success* and *include others in our partnership* are a promise to end organizational backbiting and gossip, and to communicate openly, honestly, and directly to a person, rather than talk behind their back. It has frequently been asserted that gossip destroys organizations.[lxiii] Committed partnership is the antidote to the poison that is gossip.

In this chapter, we have examined the *what* and *why* of organizational transformation. In the next chapter, we will look at the *how*.

CHAPTER SEVEN
TRANSFORMATIONAL LEADERSHIP

We have defined transformation, both personal and organizational, *as a shift in the locus of identity from content to context*. Said another way, transformation occurs when an entity (an individual, a relationship, or an organization) sees itself not as an object or a victim being acted upon by powers greater than itself but as the space in which the content or circumstances of life occur.

As for leadership, definitions abound, but one that I think sums it up well is from an article in *Forbes* by the author Kevin Kruse: "Leadership is a process of social influence, which maximizes the efforts of others, towards the achievement of a goal."[lxiv]

If we combine his definition and ours, then transformational leadership is **a *process of social influence that maximizes the efforts of an entity toward achieving and sustaining a shift from content to context.***

In organizational terms, this shift can happen at two levels:

- Interpersonal (group or team)—Two or more people shift the identity of their group from being an entity competing or collaborating with (or ignoring) other groups to being a unified voice that creates a context, for example, of high performance, equality, inclusion, or belonging.

- Systemic (organization)—A group of people take on shifting the culture of an organization from the default culture in which individuals are subject to the pressures of the culture ("the way things are done around here") and create a new culture.

Remembering Drucker's assertion that "culture eats strategy for breakfast," and Erhard's "context is decisive," we can say that organizational transformation is cultural transformation—absent cultural transformation, individual- and interpersonal-change efforts will fail.

HOW DOES TRANSFORMATION WORK?

The general rubric of organizational transformation has four parts:

1. Examination of the organization's default context and how it is working in today's environment.

   Example: We have always depended on new business through referrals. That's how the organization started, but it's no longer working.

2. Recognition of what the default context has cost the organization in productivity, ROE, employee turnover, and engagements, etc.

   Example: Our lack of diversity is costing us business, and employees from historically marginalized groups have a very high turnover rate.

3. Creation of a new and more desirable culture and translation of this into new organizational vision, mission, and values.

Example: We are committed to a culture of diversity, equity, inclusion, belonging, and justice.

4. Creation of and commitment to a body of cultural practices that are consistent with the new culture and displace those old practices that are unproductive or inconsistent with the values.

Example: Adopting and committing to values such as equity, compassion, justice, anti-racism…

THE ROLE OF LEADERSHIP IN ORGANIZATIONAL TRANSFORMATION

It is important at this point to be clear that, while many parts of an organization's work can be *managed*, transformation must and can only be *led*.

In *The Essential Drucker*, Peter Drucker defined management as "the practice of enabling groups of people with different knowledge, skills, and backgrounds to work together toward a common goal."[lxv] Elsewhere, Drucker is quoted as saying:

> *The task of management, therefore, is to make people capable of joint performance, to make their strengths effective and weaknesses irrelevant. In other words, the fundamental role of the manager is to get work done through others, and not just through a few others, but getting many people together to jointly perform organizational goals.*[lxvi]

These statements are very different from, for example, Kruse's definition of leadership with which we began this chapter. Drucker and others who study management place the emphasis on processes and outcomes. The emphasis on balancing out weaknesses by amassing complementary strengths omits the development of people and ignores attitudes, engagement, etc. We could see this as a hold-over from Frederick Taylor (see chapter six), where workers are seen as (often reluctant) interchangeable parts, and management's job is to get the most out of them for the good of the company.

Looking again at Kruse's definition—**Leadership is a process of social influence, which maximizes the efforts of others towards the achievement of a goal**—we still see the orientation toward the end result (the goal), but with the emphasis on "social influence" to "maximize the efforts of others." In an organization that has taken on a commitment to transformation, this means the creation of a context in which the means is influence, rather than authority, and workers' efforts are maximized by means other than the proverbial carrot-and-stick approach.

Management, in the inherited paradigm of organization that we described in chapter six, has always been based on position and authority—ultimately on force. In his book *Power vs. Force*, David Hawkins points out a largely unexamined aspect of force:

> *While there may be nuanced differences, I will use force to mean the entire spectrum from implicit authority to direct threat, namely that force always creates counterforce; its effect is to polarize rather than to unify. Polarization always implies conflict; its cost, therefore, is always high. Because force incites polarization, it inevitably produces a win/lose dichotomy.[lxvii]*

Force is inextricably tied to hierarchy—each level of the organizational structure has its own level of authority, and that authority is always focused downward. Endeavoring to move up the ladder is based in part on increasing one's authority or span of control, as well as on accumulating money and prestige, each of which carry their own inherent force. Authority is the currency of hierarchy, and like any currency, its value lies in the perception that it is a scarce commodity to be hoarded and conserved.

In their book *The Seven Laws of Enough: Cultivating a Life of Sustainable Abundance*,[lxviii] my colleagues Gina LaRoche and Jennifer Cohen, the founders of Seven Stones Leadership, make a convincing case that scarcity is a myth that has persisted throughout much of human history in service of hierarchical structures such as patriarchy, uneven distribution of wealth, and even happiness. Scarcity creates cultures of haves and have-nots.

Power, on the other hand, does not create its own opposition—it is *inclusive* rather than *exclusive*. Because it creates polarization and conflict, force is rooted in the primitive responses of the amygdala, and it confines the person to fight, flee, freeze, or appease responses. Power, on the other hand, is liberating. The legal scholar Charles Reich put it this way:

> *Power means to me pretty much the same thing as freedom. Power is a thing that everybody wants the most that they can possibly have of. That is, skiing is power; sex appeal is power; the ability to make yourself heard by your congressman is power. Anything that comes out of you and goes out into the world is power, and in addition to that, the ability to be open, to appreciate, to receive love, to respond to others, to listen to music, to understand literature, all of that is power. By "power" I mean human faculties exercised to the largest possible degree. So in a way, in a large sense, by power I mean individual intelligence. Now, when you reach out to another person through the energy or creativity that is in*

you, and that other person responds, you are exercising power. When you make somebody else do something against their will, to me that is not power at all; that is force, and force to me is the negation of power.[lxix]

My fifty years' experience in organizational transformation has consistently demonstrated that when we talk about organizational transformation, we are talking about leadership. Leading organizational transformation breaks down like this:

- The top executive in the organization[lxx] must be the champion for designing a new culture. In one organization I worked with a few years ago, we were brought in by the CEO's chief of staff, with assurances that the CEO was 100 percent behind the effort. We met with the CEO and explained the process, including that they must understand that the middle stages of the work would get messy. But, when it got messy, the CEO stood behind their "trusted chief of staff" and was not as solidly behind the initiative as we were led to believe. The initiative failed, and the people who were invested in the promise that transformation carried left the organization.

   Why "messy"? There is a mistaken belief that transformational change happens magically, just as the fairy godmother transformed Cinderella from a raggedly dressed, dirt-smudged servant into a princess in a gown and glass slippers. Nothing could be further from the truth. A common metaphor for transformation is that of a lowly caterpillar becoming a majestic butterfly—technically from the larval (caterpillar) through the pupal to the adult (butterfly) stages. In fact, during the larval stage, the caterpillar's body essentially liquefies and reforms into the adult butterfly. This stage can last from a few days to several weeks, depending on the species.[lxxi]

*The dissolution is gooey, messy, and seemingly chaotic. Inter-
fere or interrupt the process, and there will be no butterfly.*

In his book Work with Source,[lxxii] *Tom Nixon attributes the term "source" to the economist Peter Koenig, though
it is very difficult to find anything directly attributable to
Koenig. He defines the role of "source" is to "activate
the human ability to imagine a future which does not yet
exist and then manifest it in reality." As we will see later
in this chapter, the role of a transformational leader is to
create futures through language; in Nixon's terms, to "source"
futures that are not predictable from history or past performance. Organizational transformation needs a source,
ideally the person in the top role.*

- Top executives must communicate their commitment to transform the culture in a number of ways:

  ◊ By taking a bold stand on behalf of the future that is
  being created.

  ◊ By aligning the top leadership of the organization around
  that bold stand such that those leaders are intellectually
  and emotionally committed to creating that future and are
  in partnership with the top executive, forming what we will
  call the executive leadership team (ELT). The ELT is the
  engine that drives the transformation.

  ◊ By sponsoring the organization-wide communication
  of the new future and the cultural principles (see chapter
  eight) that will create and sustain it. This communication
  is *informative* to ensure that everyone is included in and
  understands the nature of and reasons for the new culture
  and also *committed* in that it is a request from the ELT

that looks for a response (promise) from the organization to take on the practices, over time, in community.

◊ By holding themself and others accountable to "walk the talk" of the cultural practices, the ELT creates and adopts.

- Top executives must educate and train middle management to take the lead in the day-to-day implementation of the new culture. A great deal has been and continues to be written about the role of middle management in change.[lxxiii] In transformation change, if the ELT is the engine driving the institution of the new culture, middle management is the drivetrain, translating the power generated by the engine to the parts of the organization where "the rubber meets the road" and ensuring that the values and practices of the new culture are present in every interaction, both internally amongst employees and externally with customers, suppliers, and other stakeholders.

- Top executives must enforce regular and frequent processes to assess what is working in the changing environment, what needs improvement, and what is missing and needs to be introduced. These conversations need to take place at every level, and those who are implementing the changes—that is, middle management and the "shop floor" (business development, marketing, sales, manufacturing, customer service)—need to be listened to carefully, with an eye toward common biases, particularly confirmation bias and the sunk-cost fallacy.[lxxiv]

LEADERS CREATE FUTURES THROUGH LANGUAGE

Organizational transformation comes down to creating a future that is unpredictable from past history or performance, and then making it happen. As was the case with personal transformation, this happens through language.

Language is a transformational leader's most important resource. To substantiate this assertion, we must first distinguish more about the role of language in leading people and organizations.

One of the fundamental requirements of being a transformational leader is to create futures that are not predictable. Notice the use of the term "futures," versus the more common "*the* future."

The distinction between "futures" and "the future" is a simple but profound and a provocative use of language that reminds us language has two dimensions. It can be **descriptive** and used to depict conditions or artifacts that already exist in the world, such as chairs, tables, fear, excitement, etc.

Language can also be **generative** and used to create future outcomes or conditions that are not yet true and not necessarily predictable. An example of this was when President Kennedy declared that within the decade of 1960–1969, the US would land a man on the Moon and return him safely to Earth. At the time of this declaration, the technology did not exist to fulfill his promise.

In the case of transformational leadership, we ask executives not to predict the future by extrapolating from the past, but rather to generate futures *ex nihilo*—out of nothing—and informed by and aligned with certain parameters. Those can be the company's mission, past history, the market, etc., but the futures are not limited by these parameters. While we may have ideas on how to make that future a reality, circumstances (the marketplace, unions, and the economy, for example) are quite unpredictable, and therefore require executives to exercise great courage in declaring how the future is going to turn out.

Leaders must speak for, listen for, and evoke action on behalf of a compelling future or many futures. They must ignite the passion and strategic action of their employees to deliver results that will fulfill those futures.

We could say that a vision will be fulfilled through thousands of conversations and actions that result from them, making the rigor with which leaders engage in conversation extraordinarily important. Whether those conversations are with each other, with employees, with external stakeholders, or with unions, what is said and how it is perceived matters a great deal.

We cannot discuss the role of language and effective action without understanding that to be human is to be preoccupied with MEANING. Meaning or purpose is the basic building block for being human and is an essential prerequisite to taking action. Just as we saw before that language can be either descriptive or generative, meaning is either *automatic* or *volitional*. We inherit a great deal of meaning as part of our journey from birth to death. Meaning is subjective and influenced by culture, ethnicity, family of origin, gender, religion, geography, and socioeconomic conditions. An action that has meaning in one country can have a very different meaning in another country (for example, slurping while eating soup).

Another name for meaning is "context." When you ask a person to use a word in context, you are asking them to articulate the word in a larger framework of meaning to help you understand how and why the word is being used.

What are the mindset shifts, the behavioral changes, and the daily conversations required to live, breathe, and act in a way that delivers on the vision? From the vision will be derived values, and from values, cultural practices.

However the particulars fall out, it all comes back to language. The first step is to *declare* the future. As we discussed in chapter four, a declaration is a speech act that is by its nature generative.

In the words of an anonymous Eskimo carver:

> *Words do not label things already there. Words are like the knife of the carver: they free the idea, the thing, from the general formlessness of the outside. As a [person] speaks, not only is [their] language in a state of birth, but also the very thing about which [they are] talking.* [lxxv]

So a future is declared *as a context.* You'll remember from chapter four, a context or a field is a space in which some things are more likely to occur and some less, even to the point of zero occurrence. There is a 100-percent chance that iron filings will line up in a magnetic field and a zero chance that apple seeds will. In a declared future, certain values, actions, and principles will manifest, and others won't. For example:

Declared Future	Derived Values	Derived Actions
Better, Not Bigger (McDonald's) [lxxv]	Brand elasticity More competitive pricing	Enhance existing locations Greater menu variety
A Coke Within Reach of Desire [lxxvi]	Accessibility Price elasticity	Add coin machines to the brand Expand local bottling
The World's Most Loved, Most Efficient and Most Profitable Airline [lxxvii]	Efficiency Discipline Excellence	I will demonstrate my Warrior Spirit by striving to be my best and never giving up. I will show my Servant's Heart by delivering Legendary Customer Service and treating others with respect. I will express my fun-LUVing attitude by not taking myself too seriously and embracing my Southwest Family. [lxxiii]

Figure 9 [lxxvi, lxxvii, lxxviii, lxxix]

It is important to note that in these and all examples, values are also declarations, but they differ from taking a stand in that they are derived from stands—they show up in the field of a declared future, provide guidance for the implementation of the future, and offer a way of testing whether proposed actions are consistent with the declared future. Alignment of the declared future (vision), values, and actions brings us back to *integrity* as discussed in chapter six, except now it is at an organizational level.

For individuals, as we saw in the Maliwada Training School statement in chapter six, integrity has three levels—(1) *hygiene*, keeping one's promises, etc., (2) *idealism*, being true to one's ideals, and (3) *ultimateness*, being true to oneself. Organizational integrity follows the same rubric. For an organization, ultimate integrity lies in being true to the declaration of what the organization is—for example, if McDonald's is to be better, not bigger, it would be inconsistent to make expansion a priority over new products that appeal to local tastes.

An organization's values correspond to the individuals' ideals. Costco, for example, has a strong value of customer service. To be true to this value, they have a policy that if an item goes on sale within thirty days of its having been purchased, the customer is entitled to a refund of the difference between what they paid and the sale price. In addition, they offer a guarantee of 100-percent satisfaction with anything they sell.[lxxx]

In my work on transformational change in organizations, I have found that integrity is inherently related to accountability. In chapter five, we discussed accountability as it applies to individuals. To review, the principles of accountability are:

- **Accountability is based on a promise:** Being accountable means you agree to identify yourself as the sole agent for an outcome, regardless of the unpredictability of what may happen between the time you make the promise and the time you commit to fulfilling it.

- **Accountability means activities aren't enough:** You've promised an *outcome*, and if you don't deliver that outcome, it won't matter how hard you tried or how much you wanted to.

- **Accountability is neither shared nor conditional.** Accountabilities are without condition. If it's your promise, you are accountable, regardless of circumstances. Individuals must go beyond traditional "reasonableness" and use any ethical means to produce the result.

- **Accountability is meaningless without positive consequences**. Accountability is not about finding fault, assigning blame, or punishing. It is about achieving success and learning from mistakes.

These same principles apply to organizations, and in chapter eight, we will discuss the nature of a culture of accountability. For our purposes here, a critical addition to the four principles is *100-percent accountability*. The origin of this idea is unclear, though it was put forward in 2020 by John Izzo in his book *Stepping Up: How Responsibility Changes Everything*.[lxxxi]

In my work with Dr. Loretta Malandro, based on her book *Fearless Leadership*,[lxxxii] we used Izzo's idea extensively with organizations and found it to be one of the critical and most powerful tools for organizational transformation. What follows is based on that work.

In the default paradigm of organizations (and individuals as well), accountability is fifty-fifty.

> *"I did my job, so if the result didn't turn out as expected, it must be that X didn't do their job."*

This, by the way, is a subset of the larger human principle that failing to produce a result plus a good reason is the functional equivalent of producing the result.[lxxxiii]

> *"You're late."*

> *"There was an accident on the freeway that tied up traffic."*

> *"Oh, okay."*

You'll recognize from this that fifty-fifty accountability is rooted in blame—blame others, blame the circumstances, or as a last resort, blame yourself ("I'm just no good at math."). Referring back to chapter three, this places fifty-fifty accountability squarely in the realm of the victim triangle.

One hundred-zero accountability is the basis of the transformation triangle of ownership/commitment/action. First of all, I made a promise (principle 1 above). I made it—no one forced me to make it. I had a choice, and I own that I made the promise—no hedging, weaseling, or nitpicking allowed. For example, when you accept a driver's license from the government, you are promising to obey the traffic laws. If you are stopped for speeding, you don't get to say, "I never promised to obey the traffic laws."

So in a context of 100-percent accountability, if the promise wasn't kept, you own it—"I'm late," not "I'm sorry I'm a little bit late; I was held up in traffic." You then state your commitment—"While I missed the mark this time, I am committed to delivering on what I promise in the future." Finally, you take the appropriate action—"Please tell me what the impact was of my not keeping my promise and how I can make up for it." (This is called "cleaning up" and will be covered in detail in chapter eight.)

To summarize, in organizational transformation, the job of leadership is to:

- Envision or align with the new future being created for the organization and its stakeholders. That is, create the (new) purpose of the organization.

- Establish the mission—the actions that will fulfill the new future, For McDonald's, it was a shift from wholesale expansion to improved product quality and variety.

- Articulate the organization's values that will guide everyone from the executive suite to the shop floor in having their actions be an expression of that purpose and mission.

> *In one of my first organizational consulting jobs, I was working with a company that specialized in facilitating the relocation of employees who needed to move as a result of their job. The company was called Premier Relocation, which no longer exists, but it is apparently a common name in that industry—this story does not refer to any company existing in 2024.*
>
> *In the course of our work, the company adopted a new paradigm of excellence. At that time, the work of Gary Hamel and C.K. Prahalad on Strategic Intent[lxxxiv] was very popular, and the company adopted as their strategic intent the expression "every move premier" and communicated it widely to the organization.*
>
> *As I was leaving their office late one evening, I was waiting for the elevator, and the janitor came by, sweeping the floor in*

the elevator lobby. As a test, I asked him how "every move premier" showed up in his work. Without missing a beat, he gave several careful sweeps of his mop and said with a grin, "See? Every move—premier." That was when I knew the work that I was doing was working.

- Create cultural practices as a benchmark for people to gauge whether behavior or actions—past, present, or contemplated—are consistent with the organization's purpose, mission, and values.

- Examine progress frequently with an eye toward adjusting, improving, and maintaining what is working, fixing or eliminating what is not working, and creating what is needed.

Finally, as Denise Lee Yohn pointed out in the *Harvard Business Review* article "Company Culture is Everyone's Responsibility," the traditional top-down approach to building company culture no longer works. A new culture-building approach has arisen, one in which everyone in the organization is responsible for it. "Importantly, this model doesn't relegate culture-building to an amorphous concept that everyone influences but no one leads or is accountable for. And it weaves in perspectives from employees to customers, from middle managers to the CEO."

In the next chapter, we will look at organizational cultures of transformation—creating, maintaining, and sustaining them.

CHAPTER EIGHT
SUSTAINING ORGANIZATIONAL TRANSFORMATION

As with personal transformation, organizational transformation is a practice, not an event. Both forms of transformation are sustained by *practice, over time, in community* (see chapter five).

THE ROLE OF SOURCE

In the last chapter, we noted the importance of leadership from the top of the organization, and particularly from the CEO. By taking a bold stand for the transformation, the CEO becomes the "source"[lxxxvi] of the new, often seemingly impossible future that organizes the transformation. As we noted in chapter seven, Tom Nixon states the source's role is to "activate the human ability to imagine a future which does not yet exist and then manifest it in reality."[lxxxvii] He notes that all organizations are underpinned by a "creative field"—what we have referred to as *context*. As we've noted, in the absence of a declared or created context, organizations operate based on a default context of fifty-fifty accountability, reasons versus results, hierarchical command and control, and resistance to new ideas, particularly those that are NIH (not invented here).

The institution of a new context births a creative field. As we saw in chapter one, the effect of any field—magnetic, gravitational, or cultural—makes certain practices and events more likely to happen and others less likely. Frederick Laloux, in his book *Reinventing Organizations*, says:

> *Organizations are viewed as an independent energy field with a purpose that transcends its stakeholders. In this paradigm, we don't own or run the organization; instead, we are its stewards, listening to where it needs to go and helping it do its work in the world,*[lxxxviii]

The independent energy field that Laloux refers to is the context underlying the organization's being, and as we have noted, it is either there by default or by design. The job of the CEO as the source of the organization's creative field or context is first to declare it, then to gain alignment on it, and finally to institute the cultural practices that will sustain it.

CULTURAL PRACTICES

In addition to declaring the vision for the future as a bold stand, the CEO puts in place and stands for cultural practices. *Cultural practices* are the traditional and customary practices of a particular ethnic or cultural group.[lxxxix] Used in reference to organizational transformation, cultural practices are neither traditional nor customary but rather are designed to put the values that derive from the vision into day-to-day practice within the organization.[xc] Cultural practices are the practice element of practice, over time, in community. John Ryan, then CEO of Farm Credit Canada and subsequently of RaboAgrifinance and of RaboBank NA, worked with a team from Malandro Consulting, of which I was a part, creating brilliant results when he declared that FCC would be a high-performance organization. In a foreword to a special edition of Loretta Malandro's book *Say It Right the First Time*, he said:

> *The purpose of cultural practices is to bring everyone together with a common language, a shared understanding, and mutual skills to give us speed, agility, and sustainable results. By focusing on how we needed to work together, both internally and externally, I knew we could harness our collective intelligence and strength to gain a powerful competitive edge.*[xci]

Ryan went on to list the cultural practices of his organization:[xcii]

> *Below are Farm Credit's 10 cultural practices with a brief description of each. To the uninitiated, these may sound like jargon. At FCC, however, these words have a collective and powerful meaning. They are a shorthand communication for collaborating with speed and efficiency. More than that, our cultural practices have unleashed the discretionary effort of people to excel.*
>
> *We hold ourselves and each other accountable for our impact on business results and our impact on people. We value not just what business results are achieved but how they are achieved. We hold ourselves and each other accountable for our impact on people and for bringing the appropriate urgency, commitment, and leadership required to excel at everything we do.*
>
> *We hold ourselves and each other accountable for delivering on commitments, agreements, and promises. We accept*

accountability for delivering on our commitments. Excuses, reasons, or explanations are not used to justify unacceptable performance. When we must alter a commitment, we do this in a responsible manner and include the appropriate people.

We hold ourselves and each other accountable for building and sustaining committed partnerships. We build strong strategic alliances and partnerships both within our organization and with external partners. If our partners do not experience us as being (1) committed to their success, and/or (2) being easy to work with, we take immediate corrective action.

We hold ourselves and each other accountable for creating a safe environment where people can speak up without fear. We create a safe environment where everyone can speak up without fear of repercussion. We are committed to ensuring that our behavior fosters this type of environment, and when it does not, we immediately clean up any damage and rebuild the relationship.

We measure our success by how others perceive and respond to our leadership, not by our personal point of view. We measure our success by what others say, not our personal opinion. We do not defend, justify, or argue about how others perceive or experience our leadership. Our commitment is to being responsible for how we impact others, not to "being right."

We talk straight in a responsible manner. We are open, honest, and forthright in our discussions, and we do not irresponsibly "dump" our opinions or point of view on others.

We communicate in a way that strengthens and forwards the partnership.

We "listen for" contributions and commitment. We do not "listen against" people or ideas. We practice "listening for" the commitment, contribution, and/or intention of the communicator rather than attacking, judging, or reacting to what we think we are hearing. We do not assume that what we "heard" is what the person "said."

We are open to coaching. We actively seek and listen to coaching. We check our egos at the door and trust our partners to coach us and point out our blind spots. We proactively seek coaching.

We clean up and recover quickly. When we fail to live up to our cultural practices on a daily basis, we take immediate action to correct our behavior and to clean up our impact on others. Our focus is on quick recovery, not perfection.

We acknowledge others often and celebrate both small and large successes. Our commitment is to fostering an environment where people feel valued, safe, and inspired to do their best. We deeply value and respect the contributions and talents of others and want each person and group to know how they are making a difference.

John Ryan is the model of a generative CEO—he understands deeply that his role is to create the future, not to simply wait for it to show up. In the work he describes above, he took his organization from a default culture that was yielding success and good results to a designed culture of high performance.

PURPOSE VS. GOALS: MOVING FROM DEFAULT TO DESIGN

We can summarize at this point that an organization committed to the practice of transformation is *purpose-driven* and *values-guided*. The purpose of the organization is its vision or context—the **why** of its existence. The values are the **how**. Values set the guardrails outside of which the organization will not go. Organizations that are not committed to transforming—that are operating from the default paradigm of organization—are usually *mission-driven*. In fact, if you look at what most organizations call their vision or purpose, you will find it is more often a mission and a set of goals to be achieved.

Indeed, this is a key point that distinguishes organizations operating from a designed paradigm, as compared to those using a *default paradigm*. Simply put, purpose is *a place to come from*.

Organizations in transformation still have goals, KPIs, and results to achieve, but these are set from the organization's purpose and are subject to being changed, adjusted, and even dropped as the organization evolve. The dynamic tension between purpose and outcomes gives rise to paths that were not predicted at the outset. As we quoted in chapter five, this is the source of Murray's comment that:

> *The moment one commits oneself, then providence moves too. Multitudes of things occur to help that which otherwise could never be. A stream of events issues from the decision, raising to one's favor all manner of unforeseen accidents, meetings and material assistance, which no one could have dreamed would come his way.*[xciii]

While it might seem that both purposes and goals are focused on the future, the nature of the focus is markedly different. Purpose is a declaration of possibilities, whereas goals are destinations that are set to be reached. As illustrated below, purpose opens up a field of possible outcomes, a range of outcomes that could fulfill the purpose. Being purpose-driven allows for adjustment with changing circumstances, and failure to achieve milestones or subgoals along the way becomes an opportunity for learning rather than a setback. Goals, on the other hand, are preselected from the field of possible outcomes and narrow the view of the future to certain must-haves. of which a failure to achieve constitutes failure of the whole project.

Figure 10

This is an area where the usually brilliant Peter Drucker missed the boat. In his 1954 book *The Practice of Management*[xciv], he described *management by objectives* (**MBO**), a process of defining specific objectives (goals) within an organization that are set by management, who also define how to achieve each objective in sequence. Later modifications of **MBO** involve the employees, but still the process is goal-driven.

In today's fast-moving environment, particularly in the tech world, MBO has proven too slow and too narrow a view. Mark Zuckerberg, founder of Facebook, coined the phrase "move fast and break things" as the company's motto, which led to "fail fast" being adopted by many startups in the tech industry. *Fail Fast, Fail Often*, a book by Ryan Babineaux and John Krumboltz,[xcv] exemplifies this philosophy. Fail fast means to take advantage of a wide field of possible outcomes that can fulfill the organization's (or project's or team's) purpose by adopting a ready-fire-aim approach that emphasizes diving into action even though the plan may not be perfect, and then adjusting as you go, or even changing targets.

This approach is goal-driven, and it requires a reset as each goal is completed, either by success or failure. This reset is emotional and psychological for all involved, and may end up being an overall business-process reset as well. In other words, the default paradigm assumes that success will sustain itself somehow, and it's true that the culture, being the default, will ensure its own sustainability. A designed culture, on the other hand, requires that sustainability be part of the design. Noting again the struggle between the automaticity of the default and the need for practice over time of the designed, there are key pitfalls to be aware of.

PITFALLS FOR SUSTAINABILITY

There is nothing more difficult to take in hand, more perilous to conduct, or more uncertain in its success, than to take the lead in the introduction of a new order of things.
—Machiavelli, The Prince[xcvi]
(Also inscribed on Machiavelli's tomb)

PERSISTENCE OF THE DEFAULT CULTURE

Ultimately, sustaining a culture of transformation comes down to practice, over time, in community, including the practices of being purpose-driven—that is, measuring any new proposal against the organization's purpose in a values-guided manner, which means treating the values as guardrails for what is and is not acceptable organizational and personal behavior and taking the cultural practices seriously. However, on both the personal and organizational level, taking the lead in the introduction of a new order of things is not done on an even playing field. The default paradigm of organization has had thousands of years to develop and works in ways that are so ingrained that they defy observation. The following story may be apocryphal, but it has been in wide circulation for the past twenty or so years:

The distance between rails in the US is exactly 4ft and 8.5 inches. Why?

◊ *Because there is that much distance between the railroad tracks of the British Rail. Since the US railways started to build, they used the same measure in America.*

And why do they use that measure in England?

◊ *Because the first railroad cars in England were made in a workshop that produced wagons before the railroad was made. For the railway cars, they used the same chassis they used for the wagons.*

Why did the carriage chassis use this measure (4ft and 8.5 inches)?

◊ *Because the wheelbase on the chassis was adapted to the old European roads that had the width of that wheelbase.*

Why did the roads have that dimension?

◊ *Because the roads were made by Ancient Romans during their invasion. Their two-wheeled carriages (chariots) had that measure.*

And why did the Roman two-wheeled carriage have this measure?

◊ *Because they were constructed so that it was wide enough exactly, as they required two horses, side by side.*

Finally:

◊ *The US Space Shuttle has two solid-fuel tanks developed by Thiokol in Utah. Engineers who designed the tanks wanted to make them wider but were limited by the width of the rail tunnels, which were passing tanks through by train. The width of the tunnel was determined by the distance of the rails—4' 8.5".*

Conclusion: One of the most advanced examples of US technology is based on the width of the ass of the Roman horse.[xcvii]

So the default paradigm is hiding and, like the width of the Roman chariot wheelbase, will sneak in without our being aware of it. More insidious, however, are aspects of the default paradigm that are actually harmful. As we saw in chapter six, much of the default paradigm of organization can be found in the work of Frederick Taylor; Taylor's philosophy is grounded in the notion that workers are grudging with their time and effort and must be given detailed instructions and watched carefully. It would be generous to call this view biased and outdated; more likely, it was never true. That is the nature of assumption—once adopted, we interact with it as if it were a set of facts unless we are aware that we are assuming and constantly check and question our assumptions.

MISUNDERSTANDING MOTIVATION

As late as the 1960s, when I was a psychology student, scientists believed that motivation was controlled first by biological factors (hunger, thirst, sexual satisfaction) and second by external factors (rewards and punishments received subsequent to certain specific behaviors). For Taylor and his ilk, this meant that if you pay more, workers will work harder; if you hold out the possibility of an A on a test, students will study longer; if you threaten people for tardiness or for filling out a form incorrectly, they will be on time and fill out the form correctly.

In his book Drive: *The Surprising Truth About What Motivates Us,*[xcviii] Daniel Pink cites a paper by the psychologist Harry Harlow, presented at the Nebraska Symposium on Motivation in 1953, in which he describes a study wherein monkeys were given a simple mechanical puzzle with no reward, punishment, or anything else attached. On their own, the monkeys began manipulating the puzzle and soon solved it. Needless to say, this did not fit either theory of motivation. Harlow posited a third drive. "The performance of the task," he said, "provided intrinsic reward."[xcix] Simply put, the monkeys found gratification in solving the puzzle—the solution was its own reward.

Pink goes on to study the field of intrinsic motivation, beginning with the assertion that the Taylorian paradigm of "carrot and stick" is no longer valid, if it ever was. Pink cites four decades of scientific research on human motivation and concludes that business needs to catch up with science. For Pink, there are three intrinsic factors that are critical in today's world of work: purpose, autonomy, and mastery.

Purpose, as we have already explored, is what gives meaning to work and to life. As with the janitor at Premier Relocation in chapter seven, the more purpose a person finds in their work, and the more that purpose lines up with the purpose they have created for their own life, the more rewarding work will be.

Autonomy is the most anti-Taylor of the three principal intrinsic rewards. Pink asserts that the "default setting" for human beings is to be autonomous and self-directed. Unfortunately, as we saw in the chapters on personal transformation, this intrinsic drive gets stifled starting from a very early age, as we are told to "do as you're told" and "that's not possible"; the lack of ability for abstract thought locks these in as rigid rules:

> *To the as-yet unborn, to all innocent wisps of undifferenti-ated nothingness: Watch out for life.*
>
> *I have caught life. I have come down with life. I was a wisp of undifferentiated nothingness, and then a little peephole opened quite suddenly. Light and sound poured in. Voices began to describe me and my surroundings. Nothing they said could be appealed. They said I was a boy named Rudolph Waltz, and that was that. They said the year was 1932, and that was that. They said I was in Midland City, Ohio, and that was that.*

They never shut up. Year after year they piled detail
upon detail. They do it still. You know what they say now?
They say the year is 1982, and that I am fifty years old.

Blah blah blah. (Kurt Vonnegut, *Deadeye Dick*)[c]

Mastery, as Pink uses the term, is a mindset that sees your abilities as infinitely improvable. More recently, this has been called a *growth mindset*, as distinguished from a *fixed mindset*.[96] The opportunity for mastery creates an organizational atmosphere that maximizes this important piece of intrinsic motivation.

When entire companies embrace a growth mindset, their employees report feeling far more empowered and committed; they also receive greater organizational support for collaboration and innovation. In contrast, people at primarily fixed-mindset companies report more cheating and deception among employees, presumably to gain an advantage in the talent race.[ci]

SUPER-CONTEXTS

Organizational transformation can be undermined by societal or cultural contexts that operate outside the awareness of the organization. Examples of super-contexts include White supremacy, male hegemony (patriarchy), xenophobia, caste or class consciousness, gender stereotyping, and more. In my previous book, *Inclusion: The Role of Leadership*,[cii] I devoted an entire chapter to the paradigm changes required to make organizations and society itself inclusive, equitable, and just. The roots of these societal paradigms go deeper than even the millennia-old default paradigm of organization and are incorporated into individuals' survival strategies along with their distinct answers to the survival question.

In her book *The History of White People*,[ciii] Professor Nell Irvin Painter traces White supremacy in the Western world back to the Greeks and Scythians, proceeding in an unbroken line to the present day. Psychologist Carol Gilligan, in her book *Joining the Resistance*,[civ] asserts "the gender binary and hierarchy are the DNA of patriarchy—the building blocks of a patriarchal order." What Gilligan calls the gender binary—the unspoken, unquestioned assumption that there are two distinct genders that overlap minimally, if at all, along with the historic hegemony of the masculine over the feminine—is at the heart of men's historic difficulty, not to say inability, to work with women.

In the end, male hierarchical culture impacts both women and men negatively in the workplace, socially, and at home. Deborah Tannen[cv] has studied male-female interaction, and her books and videos show graphically how men talk over women, interrupt them, ignore them, and repeat what women have just said as if they never said it, implicitly claiming the woman's thinking as their own. (Much of the same behavior can be shown to occur by so-called White men toward men of color, straight men toward GBTQ men, etc.). An important result of this hierarchical culture of (White) male privilege and unconscious bias is the suppression of the contributions of women and traditionally excluded people in service to maintaining the hierarchy.

For organizational transformation to be most effective and produce the business results that are possible, it is critical that, in the effort to create a new, transformed culture, these supercontexts be dealt with, called into people's awareness, and counter behaviors outlined in the organization's values and cultural practices.

STRUCTURAL FACTORS IN ORGANIZATIONAL TRANSFORMATION

As we noted in the chapters on personal transformation, and as Heidegger stressed, *being* is inseparable from *being-in-the-world*. Thus, when an individual takes on transforming themselves, they declare a new way of being and mark outcomes that will reflect and demonstrate that new being. Organizations, as we have noted, create a new culture or paradigm and set outcomes as indicators. In both cases, "how" is an emergent property generated in the tension between "why" (the context or purpose) and "what" of in-the-world outcomes and is guided by values consistent with the new way of being.

In organizational transformation, the "how" is guided not only by the values but also by the cultural practices. In my work with organizations over the years, I have found that the creation of a new, more-humane paradigm inevitably changes how the company is organized and how it is governed, including how decisions are made.

ORGANIZATIONAL STRUCTURE AND GOVERNANCE

The hierarchical, authority-based structure of organizations has lasted for thousands of years because it is useful. In a Taylorian structure where every person has a specific task and must be monitored to ensure that they do it and do it correctly, that paradigm works. In an organization like the military, where lives and whole societies depend on fast responses and a high degree of coordination, authority and uniformity of training are at a premium.

For today's organizations and workers, however, and especially taking into account Pink's research, this model is mostly outmoded and actually detrimental to employee engagement and ultimately to progress, profitability, and sustainability. A number of alternatives to the default structure have been put forth.

As early as 1851, the French philosopher Auguste Comte[cvi] proposed, under the term "sociocracy" that a government led by sociologists would use scientific methods to meet the needs of all people, not just the ruling class. Comte's work was carried on by others into the twentieth and twenty-first centuries, culminating in the work of Gerard Endenburg and his colleague Annewiek Reijmer, who created the *Sociocratisch Centrum* (Sociocratic Center) in the Netherlands.

In the early part of the current century, Brian Robertson, founder of Ternary Software, distilled that company's best practices into an organizational system called "holacracy."[cvii] He derived the term from "holarchy," a term from Arthur Koestler's book *The Ghost in the Machine*.[cviii] Koestler theorized that a holarchy is composed of "holons" or units that are autonomous and self-reliant, but also dependent on the whole of which they are part. Thus, a holarchy is a hierarchy of self-regulating holons that function both as autonomous wholes and as dependent parts.[cix]

Robertson then went on to develop a novel organizational structure consisting of roles, circles, and processes that defined each role's and circle's authority (domain), how they were governed, and how they operated, including using a new form of decision-making called "integrative decision-making," which involves integrating different ideas until a feasible solution is reached.

A number of for-profit and not-for-profit organizations adopted and practiced holacracy, notably including Zappos[cx] and Mankind Project USA.[cxi] Zappos received quite a bit of attention for this experiment, and while the organization has reported finding it useful, they have, in recent years, modified the system. Mankind Project USA adopted holacracy in 2017, when I was chair of the organization, and then, in 2020, they modified it. In these two cases, as in others, it was reported that the system was overly rigid and difficult to apply.

One other approach worth noting is that of Frederic Laloux in his book *Reinventing Organizations*.[cxii] Laloux, a former consultant with McKinsey, recognized the need for a new paradigm for organizations and presented a vision of organizations that is more adaptable, purpose-driven, and homocentric, based on research and with examples to support the effectiveness of such models. One key that Laloux and others do not address sufficiently is the need for new models of decision-making.

DECISION-MAKING IN THE NEW CULTURE

I distinguish four basic kinds of decision-making:

- Authoritarian
- Democratic
- Consensus
- Participative

None of these is best in all situations—each has its advantages and its drawbacks. Participative decision-making, however, is best suited to the model of transformed organizations being presented here; it maximizes the contribution of everyone on a team made up of diverse competencies that is tackling complex problems or business issues.

I suggest that critical tests of decision-making are execution and engagement—how effectively and efficiently do those whom the leader is leading execute; that is, produce desirable results that move the business forward? How connected do those who are being led feel to each other, to the leader, and, most importantly, to the long-term vision or goals of the company?

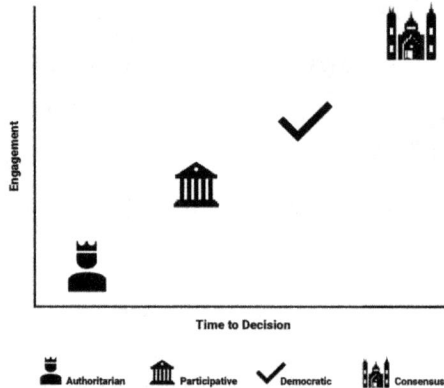

Figure 11

Authoritarian decision-making is familiar. It is the basis of the default paradigm of organizations: the leader takes charge, makes the decisions, sets the direction, and expects employees to be loyal followers. Those affected by the decision may ask questions for clarification, but not to object or point out shortcomings. From the standpoint of execution, authoritarian decision-making is fast—the only limit on it is how fast the leader makes and communicates the decision. Engagement, however, is almost always low, as those who are executing the leader's orders are disconnected from the purpose of the activity and the decision-making process. Authoritarian decision-making works best under exigent circumstances—for example, in an emergency, such as a fire, or when the consequences for nonexecution are high, such as in the military or a prison.

Democratic decision-making seems appealing. The leader gives all those involved the opportunity to vote on options, and the option receiving a majority or plurality of votes is adopted. Speed here can be high, depending on how much time is allowed for study and debate, and engagement will be high, at least for those who voted for the adopted option. Used over the long term, however, democracy has a tendency to devolve into factions and politics; as a result, the options adopted may be those with the most skilled advocates rather than the best solutions. Democratic decision-making works well when the stakes of the decision are not high and the group involved is ad hoc rather than one working together on a long-term basis.

Consensus decision-making is biased toward engagement at the expense of speed of execution and stability. The consensus-seeking leader will work with constituents to achieve 100-percent agreement. The advantages of this in terms of engagement are obvious, but there are flaws. First, seeking 100-percent common ground may result in a dilution of the options to the lowest common denominator. Second, the coalition formed is often fragile and can fall apart with any member's withdrawal of their agreement; similarly, any member can stall the process indefinitely by withholding their agreement in the first place. Consensus decision-making works best with small groups of like-minded individuals.

Participative decision-making provides the optimal combination of speed and engagement. The leader clearly communicates the relationship of the issue under discussion to the larger purpose or vision of the organization and why each person is involved. They retain the accountability for making the final decision, but to arrive at that decision, they consult with all constituents, listening to learn from differing points of view and resolving differences among them. In the end, engagement is usually high because everyone experiences having their point of view listened to, acknowledged, and appreciated. Even those whose preference was not adopted are engaged by being heard and valued.

In my experience with large corporations, participative decision-making is particularly well-suited to maximizing the value of differences in diverse teams. The leader creates a commonality of purpose while at the same time encouraging diverse views rather than pretending that differences do not exist, mining these differences for potential "gold," and maximizing the contribution of each person and group.

As noted earlier in this chapter, organizational transformation is not an event, but a practice. As with personal transformation, it will take time and will grow as awareness grows and positive results are seen. Like personal transformation, organizational transformation requires a new relationship with errors and failures—they must be treated as opportunities for learning rather than evidence that the new culture isn't working.

As Thomas Jefferson said, "eternal vigilance is the price of liberty," and nowhere is that truer than in the early stages of transformation. Practice, over time, in community, and mutual support are critical. Committed partnership (see chapter six) is the essential relationship of organizational transformation.

Finally, sustainability is key. Sustainability of the designed culture is based on clear cultural principles and practices, accountability, participative decision-making, and, above all, patience. The "over time" part in practice is critical lest we rip open the chrysalis and find we are left with a mass of goo rather than a beautiful new butterfly.

CHAPTER NINE
PRACTICING AND SUSTAINING TRANSFORMATION

AN UNEQUAL BATTLE

Transformation, whether of an individual, a group, or an organization, is a tough row to hoe, and the odds are stacked against you.

In Robert Bly's book *Iron John*,[cxiii] which is a metaphor for the male "hero's journey,"[cxiv] an adventurer comes to a king and asks, "What can I do? Anything dangerous to do around here?" That question, in some form, is where transformation begins. The adventurer could go on adventuring, quest after quest, in the same way adventurers have for ages. Instead, he senses something more—something "dangerous"—something unknown and uncertain.

Sure enough, the king replies, "Well, I could mention the forest"—where twenty others have gone and not returned—"but there's a problem. The people who go out there don't come back. The return rate is not good."

"That's just the sort of thing I like," says the adventurer, and off he goes, his little dog at his side. When he enters the forest, as he passes a pond, a hand reaches up from the pond, grabs the dog, and pulls it down. Bly notes that the adventurer doesn't get hysterical or upset; he merely says, "This must be the place," and goes back to the village and organizes a bucket party to drain the pond, at the bottom of which they find Iron John, the wild man.

Bly contends that when a person looks into their psyche, they may find another person there—a person who is untamed and has been long buried. That buried persona is Vonnegut's Rudolph Waltz before "light and sound poured in" to describe him and his surroundings.

As Freud, Jung, and others have theorized, it seems impossible to avoid the perfect storm. Before any coherent sense of self can be developed, the child must answer Berne's question: "What do I have to do to survive around here?" This is the equivalent of the adventurer asking, "Anything dangerous to do around here?" without the means to understand the question, much less its implications, nor the capacity to formulate an answer.

Instead, the perfect storm has the child default to the amygdala and its preprogrammed responses of fight, flee, freeze, or appease. Since all attributions are received as true and concrete, the child who is told "aren't you a nice boy" will appease, the one told "why do you have to struggle all the time" will fight, the one exposed to unendurable physical or emotional pain will flee, and the one who is placed in a double bind[cxv] (a communicative situation in which a person receives contradictory or conflicting messages, creating a dilemma that is difficult or impossible to resolve) is likely to freeze. By the time the child is old enough to process complex abstract input, what we call the "survival strategy" is deeply ingrained and forms the person's identity—that which the mind considers itself to be, and any suggestion that another way of seeing and relating to self, others, and circumstances is perceived as anything from "that's just not me" to a threat to survival.

Similarly, as we've seen, organizations have default cultures consisting of hierarchy, authority, information hoarding, etc., and an organizational identity that can only be changed with heroic effort. Indeed, suggesting these changes will often be met with derision, sarcasm, and dismissal, such as:

> *Everything that can be invented has been invented.*
> —Charles H. Duell, Director of US Patent Office, 1899

> *Who the hell wants to hear actors talk?*
> —Harry M. Warner, Warner Bros., c. 1927

> *Sensible and responsible women do not want to vote.*
> —Grover Cleveland, 1905

> *There is no likelihood man can ever tap the power of the atom.*
> —Robert Millikan, Nobel Prize in Physics, 1923

> *Heavier than air flying machines are impossible.*
> —Lord Kelvin, President, Royal Society, c. 1895

> *Babe Ruth made a big mistake when he gave up pitching.*
> —Tris Speaker, 1921

And those are just a sampling of many such statements.[cxvi]

When individuals in an organization attempt to transform the culture, the organization will treat the attempt in a way that is analogous to how the body treats a virus, with one of three outcomes: rejection, encapsulation, or infection. In my work, I have seen all three.

REJECTION

The CEO of a supermarket chain of over one hundred stores brought in a team of consultants who were experts in organizational transformation. Beginning with the top management, the team worked with the company to design a new culture—one of inclusion and belonging, engagement, exemplary customer service, and overall excellence. When the executive leadership team was fully and enthusiastically engaged with the transformation, the team went on to work with management, both in headquarters and in the stores, with continuing excellent results by all measures.

Then the CEO retired, and his successor decided that the changes which he had previously enthusiastically engaged in were the old CEO's thing and withdrew his support. Within a year, the company had largely reverted to its default culture.

ENCAPSULATION

A large manufacturing division of an even larger technology company was building a large new manufacturing plant outside the US. The project was behind schedule and over budget, so they brought in a consulting team to help. The team quickly determined that the root cause of the breakdowns lay not in technical issues, but in communication and collaboration within the team and between the team and other groups within and outside the company.

Changing the style of communication and collaboration within a group necessarily changes the culture. The project came in on time and on budget. This led to the head of the division engaging the team to work with the entire division, and before too long, things changed dramatically—employee engagement was up, productivity and profitability grew beyond predictions, and that division became known throughout the company's worldwide workforce as a shining example, and also as an exceptional case. "Those guys in X division are crazy—no one can duplicate what they are doing."

INFECTION

The chief human resources officer of a national bank outside the US had had an experience with a team of consultants that was very much like that of the supermarket chain described above—a major transformation effort that was enthusiastically sponsored by the CEO and that was on the verge of going viral when the CEO retired. A combination of a long interregnum with much uncertainty and the eventual appointment of a new CEO over the acting CEO, who was a proponent of transformational work, led to the HR officer's resignation and his moving to the bank, where he brought the same team in to work with the executive leadership team (ELT), with great results—the ELT including the CEO were enthusiastic and co-created a plan with the team to train divisional "champions" who would become experts in the new culture and its values and practices. It spread like a virus through the organization. This effort is still in progress, but all signs point to a successful organizational transformation.

In both the individual and the organizational cases, one conclusion offers itself as axiomatic: transformation does not happen without a struggle. People and organizations do not give up the default paradigm—whether it's the survival strategy for the individual or the default culture for the organization—easily, nor should they. In both cases, it is seen as "this is who I am—if I give this up, I'll be nothing!" And "Besides, I'm not doing so bad—look where the default paradigm has got me." And both of those statements are true.

TRANSFORMATION IS MESSY

Transformation is not a cure or a panacea at any level. People whose survival strategies have led them to serious mental illness or addiction should seek appropriate therapies and support; once they are stable and can see some daylight between who they are and their identity, transformation might be useful. But the cure for heart failure is not meditation—it might help and ease symptoms for a while, but in the end, you need to address the root cause.

Similarly, transformation is not for organizations that are failing or otherwise in trouble. The reason for this is simple: transformation is messy. Transformation, enlightenment—call it what you will—is often represented as a caterpillar turning into a butterfly, which is a particularly apt metaphor, as the metamorphosis from caterpillar to butterfly is a remarkable process that involves a complete transformation of the insect's body structure. This process, known as holometaboly or complete metamorphosis, occurs in four distinct stages: egg, larva (caterpillar), pupa (chrysalis), and imago (adult butterfly).

CATERPILLAR STAGE

The caterpillar stage is primarily focused on eating and growing. During this phase, the caterpillar hatches from an egg and begins feeding voraciously on its host plant. It grows rapidly, molting several times as it outgrows its exoskeleton. Even at this early stage, the caterpillar contains small clusters of cells called imaginal discs, which are primed to become adult features like antennae, wings, and legs.

PUPATION

When the caterpillar has grown sufficiently, it enters the pupal stage. The caterpillar finds a protected spot and molts for the final time, forming a chrysalis (not a cocoon—butterflies typically form chrysalises, while moths form cocoons). This transformation is triggered by hormonal changes, specifically a decrease in juvenile hormone levels.

INSIDE THE CHRYSALIS

The pupa stage is where the most dramatic changes occur. The caterpillar releases digestive enzymes that break down most of its body into a "tissue cell soup." This process is essentially a controlled decomposition of the caterpillar's body. The imaginal discs, which have remained dormant until now, begin to develop and differentiate. These discs use the nutrients from the broken-down larval tissues to fuel the growth of adult structures. The insect develops its adult features, including four wings, new legs, compound eyes, and reproductive organs.

EMERGENCE

After about two weeks (though this can vary by species), the fully formed adult butterfly splits open the pupal case and emerges. It hangs upside down, pumping fluid into its wing veins to expand them. Once its wings are fully expanded and dry, the butterfly is ready to fly and begin its adult life.[cxvii]

THE MESSINESS

The chief of staff to the director of a large and complex public agency became aware of transformational work through her participation with the Institute for Women's Leadership in the San Francisco Bay

Area. She came back to the agency fired up about the possibilities of taking what was one of the oldest, and in some ways most hidebound, agencies in the city's government and making it a place where people loved to work and citizens were thrilled with the service they received.

The director was skeptical at best, but wanted to encourage and empower her, so he agreed to meet with a team of consultants of which I was a member. We explained the process to him, and he thought it sounded useful and potentially valuable. We also gave him the downside—we explained, without knowing exactly what it would look like, the messiness, emphasizing not that it *might* happen, but that it *absolutely would.*

We worked with the agency for several months, and while there were individual and departmental pockets of resistance to change, by and large the work was received well, and change began to happen. At that point, the organizational immune system kicked in, attempting to reject the change. The oldest divisions of the agency resisted the hardest, citing the shopworn argument that "we've always done it this way," and invoking their longtime status as the victims of an unappreciative and undeserving public. Inevitable mistakes and breakdowns in implementing the new culture were cited as proof that it would not work, and fear of failure emerged as faintheartedness and complaining.

And it was at that point that the director learned what it was we meant when we said it would get messy. When Saddam Hussein invaded Kuwait on August 1, 1990, the American President George H. W. Bush seemed to waver. British Prime Minister Margaret Thatcher bucked him up. "Don't go all wobbly on me, George," she said. That is essentially the message we tried to convey to the director, but to no avail. The director wobbled, and the initiative foundered.

Hard-won changes were lost, and key leadership left over the subsequent year.

The lesson: Ignore the process of the chrysalis at your peril.

APPROACHES TO TRANSFORMATION

There is no "one true path" to transforming oneself or an organization. There is, however, a time-tested method that we talked about in chapter five—*practice, over time, in community*. To reiterate:

PRACTICE

- *Applying the new context through keeping the vision, mission, and values in* the forefront of awareness.

- *Catching and cleaning up mistakes—behaviors that are inconsistent with the new* context. Transformation is an art of correction, not perfection.

OVER TIME

Given the unfamiliarity of the behaviors associated with the new context and the tenaciousness of the ego's drive to survive and to reinstate the default context, practice is essential and must be carried on in the face of frustration and failure.

IN COMMUNITY

This aspect is crucial. While enlightenment may come to hermits sitting in a cave, the purpose of

transformation is to alter the quality of the person's life and, by extension, the lives of those with
whom they come into contact. This requires:

◊ That the commitment to the new context be public.

◊ *That the person, in addition to holding themselves accountable for
the new* vision, mission, and values, be willing to be held
accountable by others as well.

This method applies to individuals, but possibly more so to organizations. As we noted in chapter six, a new organizational culture and
its values must be translated into new cultural practices so that they are
not abstract concepts hung on a wall, but rather practical actions that
can be promised and managed in an atmosphere of accountability
that is guilt- and shame-free. It is one thing to say that we stand for
excellent customer service and even to have everyone take that pledge,
but then what?

Creating the new culture and its values and practices is the job
of organizational leadership, but making that culture real, on the
ground, requires management. No one is quite sure if it was Peter
Drucker or W. Edwards Deming—or someone else altogether—but
someone is frequently quoted as saying, "You can't manage what you
don't measure," and that is certainly true, regardless of who said it.
By translating values into practices—like a "we accept any returns,
whether bought here or not" policy or "all customer calls are returned
within sixty minutes" and the like—employees can be acknowledged
and appreciated for good work and corrected when they fall short.
This is PRACTICE.

In an organization, turnover is a fact of life at every level, and each
new hire, from the C-Suite to the shop floor, comes in unfamiliar
with the culture and its values and practices. They might have some

knowledge of these, but the knowledge is theoretical until they are there—in community, practicing over time.

This makes cultural education, along with leading by example, a critical part of sustaining organizational transformation, including refreshers for those who are not new. These must take place on an ongoing basis—this is OVER TIME, IN COMMUNITY—showing the value of these principles applied in organizational transformation and with individuals who make up the organization.

CHAPTER TEN
THE PITFALLS OF THE "PROMISED LAND" VIEW OF TRANSFORMATION

As we said, there is no formula for transformation—no "true path"—but there are many false ones. The past hundred or so years have seen the growth of many people, methods, and organizations that promise transformative results, and some even deliver. There are, however, a lot that don't deliver and are just money-making schemes, cults, scams, etc. Here are some red flags if you are considering undertaking one method or another. Be wary of:

- Claims to be "the only way."

- Demands for unpaid "services to an individual or organization."

- Insistence on your cutting prior ties to family, job, etc.

- Ascending levels of paying for programs.

- Insistence on particular clothing and personal grooming.

- Stories of people being prevented from leaving or being cut off if they do.

If you pick any one or two of these, it might not be a red flag—certain religious groups, for example, have dietary proscriptions, distinctive clothing, etc., but affiliation is voluntary (or even difficult) and leaving is easy. Most importantly, money is not involved or required.

One thing many "transformational" movements or organizations have in common is emphasis on proselytizing through "sharing" or "testifying" to the efficacy of one's path. This is a particularly seductive idea because, when one has a life-altering or highly impactful experience, it is natural to want to talk with others about it, both to celebrate one's own experience and to share it with others as a gift.

Sharing seems to be an inborn human drive. If I taste a particularly luscious strawberry, my first reaction is to tell you about it and offer you some so that you can have the same delightful experience that I just had. This works well with strawberries, good jokes, music, and massages. It works less well when the experience is personal and more or less ineffable. I cannot share my awe at encountering vast possibility in the same way I can share a strawberry or a dish of ice cream—I must reduce it to description. Watts said we must try to "speak the unspeakable, scrute the inscrutable, and eff the ineffable."[cxviii]

This invariably leads to difficulty, due in large part to what we will term the "poverty of description." The challenge in describing a transformative experience lies in the nature of description itself. The attempt to define or describe something presupposes that the object of description exists in some form, and that that form can be adequately captured in referential or descriptive language. But as we've seen in chapter seven, referential and descriptive language is fine for describing the present and the past, yet it is inadequate to generate futures ex nihilo.

Imagine being in Rome in the church of San Pietro in Vincoli. In the nave of the church, you encounter Michelangelo's masterpiece *Moses*. The statue itself is almost overwhelming in its dimensionality; the viewer can almost never stand in one place but must move around to capture the statue in all its aspects. As one stands before the statue for some time, details emerge that were not apparent at first, or even in a second viewing. With longer observation, one becomes aware of the lighting, the church itself, the sounds, smells, etc., as well as one's own responses to the work.

Now try to imagine describing the experience of viewing the sculpture. Even the most complete, detailed description must sacrifice the integration of the experience, and even the most careful detailing of the statue itself cannot capture the overwhelming majesty of Michelangelo's work, much less the religious, political, emotional, and all the other overtones and harmonics that cannot be described.

In the case of something that is not physical, the difficulty is much greater. Experience is not an object; it is like the statue without the physical object itself—a complex of experiences that will take form when the one who has the experiences brings them to interact with the world of physical objects and opportunities. Michelangelo, in describing creating the monumental statue of David said he could "see" (experience) the statue in the marble, and bringing that experience to interact with the stone, he is supposed to have said he "chipped away everything that was not David."

Rather than *describe* experience, one must, in conversation, paint a dimensional portrait of *the possibility*, knowing that when the conversation is over, someone who has been a bystander, observing the creation, will undoubtedly say, "Yes, but what is it?" Human experience lives in *interactivity* and is *autopoietic* in nature (that is, it is made up of systems of components that produce and maintain themselves).[cxix] The definition I found is a system's ability to reproduce and maintain itself by creating its own parts. A serious inquiry into the nature of a transformative experience will leave you with more questions than you started with.

Despite all this, if we are driven to communicate, to share something as commonplace as a strawberry, how much more are we driven to share something as profound as the experience of transformation? Because of the didactic nature of description, the experience is quickly and inevitably reduced to teaching, and teaching to dogma, or "the truth."

In the Book of Genesis, Abraham experiences the unity of God. In attempting to describe this experience, "the unity of God" subtly morphs into "there is only one God." Abraham was attempting to communicate this new idea in a polytheistic culture. A hierarchical structure of gods is characteristic of such cultures. It would be natural for their first (and perhaps only) understanding of what Abraham was saying to be that this new, solitary god of Abraham was more right, truer, or at least more powerful than Baal or Moloch, or any of their previous gods.

So, we have now gone from Abraham's experience of awe and wonder to Abraham's teaching of the "unity of God" to the doctrine of the "one true God." This, in a nutshell, is the evolution of doctrine and the devolution of experience. By virtue of the me/not me experience immediately following birth, reinforced by attributions, which continually bombard the developing child with the message that "you are over there, and the world is over here, and you have to find out how to fit into it," human beings increasingly identify themselves as a unique collection of attributes located at a specific point in space and time.

But an individual's point of view, as we have seen, is not a pure, unadulterated perception of an objective world. From birth, we accumulate ideas, experiences, and learnings that act as filters. Because this process begins long before abstract thought, much of this complex of filters is concrete. We experience it not as a point of view, but as "the way it is," and lose any sense that our experience is mediated by filters, in much the same way that we can be in an office with tinted windows and think the weather outside is turning bad unless we remember that we are seeing it through darkened glass.

So I don't have a position, a point of view—I am seeing the world *as it is.* If you see it differently, then you are either misguided, misperceiving, a fool, or a con artist. It is clear and obvious to me that my perception of the world is more right, better than, and superior to any contrary perception, and the rightness, goodness, and value of any other point of view will be a function of how close it is to mine. The wrongness, badness, and worthlessness—the otherness of any point of view other than mine becomes a threat that is measured by how far it is from my own.

- If I am a Christian, Muslim, or Jew, and you are a Buddhist, with what looks to me like no notion of a godhead, or a Hindu, with what looks to me like a polytheistic view, you are "other."

- If you are an atheist and deny the existence of a god in any form, you are even more "other," and according to the amygdala's rules, I must fight you, flee from you, be immobilized by you in the hope you will go away, or find a way to appease you so you do not harm me.

This is to be expected, of course, because language is localized in the brain in Broca's area (expression) and Wernicke's area (reception and comprehension). Both of these areas that are crucial to language are located in the left hemisphere. The "left brain" is logical, linear, and concrete in its thinking, while the "right brain" is abstract, non-linear, and touchy-feely.

If, as is our thesis, people's relationship to their experiences begins with the right hemisphere, and if, as seems apparent, the right brain, with its experience of connectedness and intuitive relationship with everyone (and everything), has a driving need to share this experience, the only medium for expressing the experience will be through the left hemisphere, in language, and so experience quite naturally expresses itself as teaching.

Yet as we discussed, even the best description is doomed to beggar the experience. But for the left brain, description is everything, and that which cannot be described cannot be real. Heidegger noted:

> *To the common comprehension, what is incomprehensible remains forever merely offensive—proof enough to such comprehension, which is convinced it was born comprehending everything, that it is now being imposed upon with an untruth and sham.*[cxx]

The result of what we can call the unconscious arrogance of the left brain is a demand for description and a discounting of that which cannot be described, and teachings are accepted as the communication of experience rather than being known for what they are—the conceptualization and symbolization of profound experience. If religion were a restaurant, the left brain would have us eating the menu instead of the meal.

Direct experience is thwarted first by the imposition of left-hemisphere logic, processional sequencing, and historic bias. The death blow to experience comes when the description that is adopted becomes masked as the truth. If what I think is wrong, then *I* am wrong. My position and the decisions I have made or adopted from others are right, good, and correct; the difference between any other position and mine is a measure of how wrong, bad, and incorrect that position is.

So, to return to the amygdala, a threat to my position is a threat to my survival, and it will be met by amygdaloid responses—fight, flee, freeze, and appease—in some combination. Further, social scientists have been aware for years that groups of like-minded individuals tend to act like individuals—that is, a threat to the group's position will be met with the same ferocity that an individual brings against a threat to their own survival.

This is the most basic scenario by which transformational experience comes to live as dogma, "right language," and cultlike aspects of "us and them." Add to that unscrupulous "teachers," and a power dynamic is created in which any challenge to the teacher is a challenge to the dogma, and in turn a challenge to the group identity and the identity of each member of the group.

This is not a small dilemma. From Abraham to Moses, to Jesus, to Buddha, to Muhammad, people who have had powerful transformative insights and experiences have been driven to teach and share what they have learned. Two universal and innate human drives contribute to this:

- Every human being is driven by the need to communicate and be understood.

- Every human being is driven by the desire to contribute.

These drives are at the basis of both the impulse to communicate and teach, and the human vulnerability of being manipulated.

One of the most dangerous and often the most subtle pitfalls of personal and organizational transformation is the subversion of the effort by leaders who are narcissistic or sociopathic personalities. Organizations that are dedicated to a higher social good seem particularly vulnerable to this because of a factor called "weaponized empathy."

Weaponized empathy is the manipulation or exploitation of empathy and emotional responses for personal gain or to advance an agenda, often in misleading or harmful ways. Some key aspects and examples include:

1. Using emotional appeals to spread misinformation or distort facts, especially on complex issues. For example, claims about electric vehicles harming children in Africa to discourage EV adoption.[cxxi]

2. Hijacking genuine concerns (like human trafficking) to push unrelated agendas or distract from real issues.[cxxii]

3. Narcissists using cognitive empathy to manipulate people (understanding others' emotions) without emotional

empathy. For example, feigning concern to gain trust before exploiting it.[cxxiii]

4. Using personal information shared in vulnerable moments for guilt-tripping or control later.

5. Corporations and advertisers leveraging empathy to sell products or ideas.[cxxiv]

6. Online trolls understanding and exploiting others' emotional responses while not experiencing those emotions themselves.

This concept highlights how empathy, while often seen as positive, can be misused as a tool for manipulation, especially in our hyper-connected world with social media and targeted advertising. It underscores the need for critical thinking alongside emotional responses. Some strategies to defend against weaponized empathy:

1. Develop critical thinking skills: Try to separate emotion from ideas and ask probing questions when presented with emotional appeals.

2. Be aware of emotional manipulation: Recognize when someone is using emotional appeals to spread misinformation or distort facts, especially on complex issues.

3. Fact-check emotional claims: Verify information, especially when it involves shocking or highly emotional content designed to provoke a strong reaction.

4. Maintain emotional boundaries: Be cautious about sharing personal information in vulnerable moments that could be used for manipulation later.

5. Recognize narcissistic tactics: Be alert to people who seem to understand your emotions but consistently steer

conversations back to themselves or use your emotions for their gain.

6. Understand the components of empathy: Recognize that true empathy involves emotional resonance, cognitive understanding, and a desire to help—not just the ability to recognize emotions.

7. Be wary of rapid emotional attachment: Be cautious of people who shower you with excessive affection or compliments very quickly in a new relationship.

8. Look for consistency in behavior: Pay attention to whether someone's empathetic behavior is consistent or if it changes dramatically once they feel secure in a relationship.

9. Seek outside perspectives: Consult trusted friends or professionals to get an objective view of situations in which you feel emotionally manipulated.

10. Educate yourself: Learn about the tactics of emotional manipulation and narcissistic behavior to better recognize and defend against them.

The goal is not to become cynical or distrustful of all empathy, but to develop a more nuanced understanding of how empathy can be misused and to protect yourself from manipulation.

The key to this is, I think, remembering to distinguish between our thoughts, feelings, interpretations, conclusions, and what is real. The transformation triangle (chapter three) begins with confronting reality as it is. The danger, in the words of an Indian philosopher, is:

Having failed to distinguish thoughts from things, we then fail to
distinguish words from thoughts. We think that if we can label
a thing we have understood it.
—Maha Sthavira Sanghakakshita

In a famous dialogue with his daughter, recounted in *Steps to an Ecology of Mind*, Gregory Bateson satirized our fascination with explanation:

Daughter (D): Daddy, what is an instinct?

Father (F): An instinct, my dear, is an explanatory principle.

D: But what does it explain?

F: Anything—almost anything at all. Anything you want it to explain.

D: Don't be silly. It doesn't explain gravity.

F: No. But that is because nobody wants instinct to explain gravity. If they did, it would explain it. We could simply say that the Moon has an instinct whose strength varies inversely as the square of the distance—

D: But that's nonsense, Daddy.

F: Yes, surely. But it was you who mentioned instinct, not I.

D: All right—but then what does explain gravity?

F: Nothing, my dear, because gravity is an explanatory principle.

D: Oh. Do you mean that you cannot use one explanatory principle to explain another? Never?

*F: Hmm…hardly ever. That is what Newton meant when he said, "*Hypotheses non fingo.*"*

D: And what does that mean? Please.

F: Well, you know what hypotheses are. Any statement linking together two descriptive statements is a hypothesis. If you say that there was a full moon on February 1st and another on March 1st; and then you link these two observations together in any way, the statement which links them is a hypothesis.

D: Yes—and I know what "non" means. But what's "fingo"?

F: Well—"fingo" is a late Latin word for "make." It forms a verbal noun fiction from which we get the word "fiction."

D: Daddy, do you mean that Sir Isaac Newton thought that all hypotheses were just made up like stories?

F: Yes—precisely that.

D: But didn't he discover gravity? With the apple?

F: No, dear. He invented it.

D: Oh…Daddy, who invented instinct?

F: I don't know. Probably biblical.

D: But if the idea of gravity links together two descriptive statements, it must be a hypothesis.

F: That's right.

D: Then Newton did fingo a hypothesis after all.

F: Yes—indeed he did. He was a very great scientist.

D: Oh.

D: Daddy, is an explanatory principle the same thing as a hypothesis?

F: Nearly, but not quite. You see, a hypothesis tries to explain some particular something, but an explanatory principle— like gravity or instinct—really explains nothing. It's a sort of conventional agreement between scientists to stop trying to explain things at a certain point.

D: Then is that what Newton meant? If gravity explains nothing but is only a sort of full stop at the end of a line of explanation, then inventing gravity was not the same as inventing a hypothesis, and he could say he did not fingo any hypotheses.

F: That's right. There's no explanation of an explanatory principle. It's like a black box.

D: Oh. Daddy, what's a black box?

F: A black box is a conventional agreement between scientists to stop trying to explain things at a certain point. I guess it's usually a temporary agreement.

D: But that doesn't sound like a black box.

F: No—but that's what it's called. Things often don't sound like their names.

D: No.

F: It's a word that comes from the engineers. When they draw a diagram of a complicated machine, they use a sort of shorthand. Instead of drawing all the details, they put a box to stand for a whole bunch of parts and label the box with what that bunch of parts is supposed to do.

D: So a black box is a label for what a bunch of things are supposed to do…

F: That's right. But it's not an explanation of how the bunch works.

D: And gravity?

F: Is a label for what gravity is supposed to do. It's not an explanation of how it does it.

D: Oh. Daddy, what is an instinct?

F: It's a label for what a certain black box is supposed to do.

D: But what is it supposed to do?

F: Hmm. That is a very difficult question…

D: Go on.

F: Well, it's supposed to control—partly control—what an organism does.

D: What did you mean by "partly control"?

F: Well, if an animal falls down a cliff, its falling is controlled by gravity. But if it wiggles while falling, that might be due to instinct.[cxxv]

So the fundamental practice (over time, in community) of transformation is to continually attempt to confront the world as it is. And as we quoted e.e. cummings in chapter 5, "if, at the end of your first ten or fifteen years of fighting and working and being, you find you've written one line of one poem, you'll be very lucky indeed… Does this sound dismal? It isn't. It's the most wonderful life on earth, or so I feel.

EPILOGUE
DREAM BIG!

Dream no small dreams for they have
no power to move [people's] hearts.
—Johann Wolfgang von Goethe[cxxvi]

Those who dream by night in the dusty recesses of their minds
wake in the day to find that all was vanity; but the dreamers
of the day are dangerous [people], for they may act their
dream with open eyes, and make it possible.
—T. E. Lawrence, Seven Pillars of Wisdom[cxxvii]

In elementary school, I had a music "teacher"—call her Miss Davenport. I put "teacher" in quotes because, in my case at least, teaching was not on her agenda. Instead, she told me I was not musical, could not sing, and should just mouth the words when the class sang together.

Remember Rudolf Waltz in the quote from Kurt Vonnegut's *Deadeye Dick* in chapter eight?

To the as-yet unborn, to all innocent wisps of undifferenti-
ated nothingness: Watch out for life.

I have caught life. I have come down with life. I was
a wisp of undifferentiated nothingness, and then a little

peephole opened quite suddenly. Light and sound poured in. Voices began to describe me and my surroundings. Nothing they said could be appealed. They said I was a boy named Rudolph Waltz, and that was that. They said the year was 1932, and that was that. They said I was in Midland City, Ohio, and that was that.

They never shut up. Year after year they piled detail upon detail. They do it still. You know what they say now? They say the year is 1982, and that I am fifty years old.

Blah blah blah.[cxxviii]

Where Miss Davenport was concerned, Vonnegut's scenario really took. I attempted to learn to play flute and to play drums and was unsuccessful at both. My singing was a standing joke amongst my family and friends. I was *not* musical. I love to listen to all kinds of music, but I myself am not musical. In college, I joined the folk song club—my ticket in was my prodigious memory for lyrics. I could carry the song when others forgot the words, and so my voice was tolerated until others remembered and joined in.

In 2013, I participated in the late Tracy Goss's Executive Reinvention Program, which was based on her book *The Last Word on Power*.[cxxix] The ERP, as we called it, was an unusual program for executives, as it combined Tracy's expertise in transformation with her love for and knowledge of theater. In addition to learning, the ERP had a practice element to it—each participant was assigned a song or speech to prepare and perform "at the level of a Broadway performance."

Remember, the majority of people in the program were corporate executives with no background or training in performing, and the assignment was not a metaphor. At the end of the program, Tracy rented a small theater (not on Broadway, but in Manhattan), guests were invited, and the performances ensued.

My assignment was "Some Enchanted Evening" from Rodgers and Hammerstein's *South Pacific*. To add to the challenge, through a misunderstanding, I was not given my song until the start of the second week of the program (the program took place over two weeks, about six weeks apart, so participants had time to prepare, hire a coach, etc.). So there I was, nonmusical me—a "mouther," per Miss Davenport—having to learn this song in four days and deliver a Broadway-level performance.

Tracy made coaches available for the performance part of the ERP, and Jimmy DePaiva, John Herrera, and Marion Cantone worked me hard that week. On Thursday evening, I took the stage and delivered the song without missing a note. Since then, I sing.

I tell this story not to try to get hired as a singer, but because it contains all the elements of transformation that we have covered in this book. My first step was to shed the messages from Miss Davenport and others that I "couldn't sing." I then declared the possibility of not just singing but performing at a professional level. I practiced over the four days, and I did so in community—with my coaches and in rehearsal sessions with the rest of the class—and I fulfilled on the possibility I had declared.

Now, in this small area, my life is changed—I have a new context for my life called singing. One evening on the ferry from Bainbridge Island, Washington, to Seattle, a couple were playing "The Skye Boat Song" on a guitar and recorder—not a performance, just passing the time. I (of course) knew the words and spontaneously sang along with their playing. When the song was done, the rounds of applause we got from the other passengers were as big as the smiles on our faces.

My colleague and friend Rayona Sharpnack, another expert in personal and organizational transformation, used to say that all it takes to make a difference is "courage and a mouth." Brené, in her seminal TED Talk "The Power of Vulnerability,"[cxxx] points out that the root of the word "courage" is the Latin "*cor*," meaning heart, and she goes on to define courage as "speaking yourself with your whole heart"—where I believe Rayona's "mouth" comes in.

Transformation begins with the self-empowering declaration "I declare that I can declare," or in more familiar language, "I am who I say I am—I am limited only by what I am unwilling to declare possible." From there, dare to dream! If I can sing, you can cast off the limits imposed on you by your premature decisions about yourself, other people, and the world.

Theodor Herzl, one of the founders of the State of Israel, said, "If you will it, it is not a dream."[cxxxi] For the abstract "will," I would substitute "declare," but the meaning is the same.

In my now fifty-year career as a psychologist, coach, and designer and deliverer of transformational programs for individuals and organizations, I have seen the impossible happen again and again through awareness, declaration of a new possibility, practice of new behaviors over time in community, and I've experienced it myself. Programs for individuals such as the Landmark Forum, the New Warrior Training Adventure, Lifespring, and others kick-start the process. Organizational leaders who are more committed to creating the future than improving on the past have led organizations I and others have worked with, making them innovative, creative, and great places to work.

To again quote Goethe, "Whatever you can do or dream you can, begin it. Boldness has genius, power, and magic in it."

ACKNOWLEDGMENTS

The trouble with acknowledgments is that they can never be sufficiently comprehensive. This book is the product of (quite literally) a lifetime of study, mentorship, training, mistakes, and learnings. Naturally, a great many people have contributed to this journey, and I am going to leave some out—not because I intend to, but because it's inevitable.

First of all, my wife, Emy, who has been enormously supportive of my work for over forty years together, and my children and grandchildren. My collaborator, editor, designer, marketer, and especially my friend, Kristine (Kriz) Bell of By Friday Media took this book into her very capable hands, and relieved me of everything except thinking and writing, while recreating my intentions brilliantly. And Halo Publications, publisher of my last book and this one, for being great about producing a quality product.

A lifetime dedicated to learning means a lifetime populated by teachers. Some of those teachers were subjects of study and didn't ever know it—this includes all my patients when I was a psychotherapist, as well as all my coaching and organizational clients. As for those who knew they were my teachers, I am deeply grateful to Marian Weisberg and Mary Boulton, who trained me in transactional analysis; Joe Wysong, who trained me in gestalt therapy; and in my consulting years, Loretta Malandro, Tracy Goss, Mickey Connolly,

Rayona Sharpnack, and a host of others. Colleagues who were instrumental in my thinking and development include Neil Rodgers, Jimmy DePaiva, Harry Sloofman, Juan Mobili, Ed Atkinson (to whom this book is dedicated), Craig Clark, Marlene Clark, Brett Morris, to name a few.

Finally, I must acknowledge my late parents, who, while they never quite understood what I was doing, had complete confidence in my ability to do it.

BIBLIOGRAPHY

Austin, J. L. *How to Do Things with Words: The William James Lectures Delivered at Harvard University in 1955*. Oxford University Press, 2009.

Babineaux, R., and J. D. Krumboltz. *Fail Fast, Fail Often: How Losing Can Help You Win*. Jeremy P. Tarcher/Penguin, 2013.

Bach, Richard. *Illusions: The Adventures of a Reluctant Messiah*. Delacorte Press. 1977.

Bateson, G. *Steps to an Ecology of Mind: Collected Essays in Anthropology, Psychology, Evolution and Epistemology*. Intertext Books, 1972.

Bateson, G., et al. "Toward a Theory of Schizophrenia." *Behavioral Science* 1 (1956): 251–264.

Becker, C. L. *Freedom and Responsibility in the American Way of Life; Five Lectures Delivered on the William W. Cook Foundation at the University Of Michigan, December 1944*. Vintage Books, 1965.

Berne, E. *Games People Play*. Puffin, 2010.

Berne, E. *What Do You Say after You Say Hello?* Corgi, 2018.

Bly, R. *Iron John: A Book about Men—25th Anniversary Edition*. Da Capo Press, 2015.

Boudreaux, G. "Peter Drucker's Continuing Relevance for Electric Cooperatives." *Management Quarterly*. 4th ed. (2005):15, 18–32.

Brown, B. "The Power of Vulnerability." April 26, 2024. *YouTube*. https:// www.youtube.com/results?search_query=brene%2Bbrown%2Bvulnerability%2Bted%2Btalk.

Brown, B. "Adding Shame, Guilt, Humiliation, Embarrassment..."..." March 4, 2024. https://brenebrown.com/wp-content/uploads/2021/09/Integration-Ideas_Emotional-Vocabulary_092221-1.pdf.

Buonarroti, M. "A Quote by Michelangelo Buonarroti." March 8, 2024. Goodreads. https://www.goodreads.com/quotes/10320211-i-created-a-vision-of-david-in-my-mindand#:~:text=Sign%20Up%20Now-,I%20created%20a%20vision%20of%20David%20in%20my%20mind%20and,everything%20that%20was%20not%20David.

"Butterfly Life Cycle." August 31, 2024. For Educators. https:// www.floridamuseum.ufl.edu/educators/resource/butterfly-life-cycle/.

"Butterfly Metamorphosis." August 31, 2024. American Museum of Natural History. https://www.amnh.org/exhibitions/butterflies/metamorphosis.

Campbell, J. "The Hero with a Thousand Faces." Joseph Campbell Foundation, 2020.

Carpenter, E. "The Eskimo Language." *ETC: A Review of General Semantics 25*, no. 4 (1968): 467–473. doi:https://www.jstor.org/stable/42574505.

Clark, C. "Fundamental of the Week #3: Speak Straight, Respectfully, SPEAK STRAIGHT, RESPECTFULLY." March 21, 2024.

https://www.momentumconsulting.com/blog/ fundamental-week-3-speak-straight-respectfully?rq=communication.

Comte, A., and H. Martineau. *The Positive Philosophy of Auguste Comte.* Kegan Paul, Trench, Trübner & Company, 1853.

Connolly, M., and R. Rianoshek. *The Communication Catalyst: The Fast (but Not Stupid) Track to Value for Customers, Investors, and Employees.* Dearborn Trade Publishing, 2002.

Covey, S.R. *First Things First: To Live, to Love, to Learn, to Leave a Legacy.* Covey Leadership Center, 1994.

Cummings, e.e. *A Miscellany*, edited by G. J. Firmage. Liveright Publishing Corporation, a division of W. W. Norton & Company, 2018.

de Ropp, R. S. *The Master Game.* Delacorte, 1968.

Dispenza, Joe. *Becoming Supernatural: How Common People are Doing the Uncommon.* Carlsbad, California : Hay House, Inc., 2019. ".

Dobelli, R. *The Art of Thinking Clearly*. Hodder and Stoughton, 2014.

Drucker, P. *Practice of Management.* Harper & Row, 1954.

Drucker, P. F. *The Essential Drucker: The Best of Sixty Years of Peter Drucker's Essential Writings on Management.* Harper, 2014.

Durant, W. *The Story of Philosophy: The Lives and Opinions of the World's Greatest Philosophers.* Pocket Books, 1926.

Dusay, J. "Script Drama Analysis." Transactional Analysis Bulletin 7, no. 26 (1968).

Dweck, C. "What Having a 'Growth Mindset' Actually Means." April 25, 2021. *Harvard Business Review*. https://hbr.org/2016/01/what-having-a-growth-mindset-actually-means.

Elmore, B. J. *Country Capitalism How Corporations from the American South Remade our Economy and the Planet.* University of North Carolina Press, 2023.

Erhard, W. "Epistemological and Contextual Contributions of EST to General Systems Theory," a preprint. Symposium on Evolving Trends in General Systems Theory and the Future of the Family. 1976.

Erhard, W. "Werner Erhard—A World That Works for Everyone." March 12, 2024. *YouTube*. https://www.youtube.com/watch?v=dTkGZq6mhJI.

Finkelstein, N. H. *Theodor Herzl: Architect of a Nation*. Lerner Publications Company, 1991.

Flavell, J. H. The Developmental Psychology of Jean Piaget. New York: Van Nostrand, 1963, 85.

Flores, F. "Conversations for Action and Collected Essays: Instilling a Culture of Commitment in Working Relationships." Createspace, 2013.

Frankl, V. E., H. S. Kushner, and W. J. Winslade. *Man's Search for Meaning*. Beacon Press, 2006.

Friedman, M. "Milton Friedman." *The Profit Doctrine*, (2016): 55–77. doi:10.2307/ j.ctt1jktsbd.9.

Gilligan, C. *Joining the Resistance*. Polity Press, 2013.

Gladwell, M. *Outliers*. Manjul Publishing House, 2015.

Goleman, D. *Emotional Intelligence*. Bloomsbury, 1996.

Goss, T. *Last Word on Power*. Rosetta Books, 2010.

Gribbin, J. *Iron John: A Book about Men by Robert Bly*. Vintage Books, 1991a.

Gribbin, J. *Iron John: A Book about Men by Robert Bly*. Vintage Books, 1991b.

Gribbin, J. *Iron John: A Book about Men by Robert Bly*. Vintage Books, 1991c.

Gribbin, J. *Iron John: A Book about Men by Robert Bly*. Vintage Books, 1991d.

Groth, A. "Zappos Has Quietly Backed Away from Holacracy." Yahoo! Finance. April 25, 2024. https://finance.yahoo.com/news/zappos-quietly-backed-awayholacracy-090102533.html.

Gurowitz, E. M. *Inclusion, the Role of Leadership: Why We Are Separate, Why We Need to Come Together*. Halo Publishing International, 2019.

Hamel, G., and C. K. Prahalad. *Strategic Intent*. Harvard Business Review, 2010.

Harbott, K. "The History of Hierarchies." March 16, 2024. Agile Centre. https:// www.agilecentre.com/resources/article/the-history-of-hierarchies/.

Hawkins, D. R. *Power vs. Force: The Hidden Determinants of Human Behavior*. Hay House, Inc., 2014.

Heidegger, M. *What Is Called Thinking?* Harper & Row, 1968.

Heidegger, M. *Being and Time*, original ed. Must Have Books, 2021.

Heidegger, M., J. Macquarrie, and E. S. Robinson (2019) *Being and Time*. Martino Fine Books, 2019.

"How Does a Caterpillar Turn into a Butterfly?" August 31, 2024. *Discover Wildlife*. https://www.discoverwildlife.com/animal-facts/insects-invertebrates/how-does-a-caterpillar-turninto-a-butterfly.

Hübl, Thomas, and Julie Jordan Avritt. *Healing Collective Trauma*. Boulder, CO: Sounds True, 2020.

Izzo, J. B. *Stepping Up: How Taking Responsibility Changes Everything*. Berrett-Koehler Publishers, Inc., 2020.

Jensen, M. C. "Integrity: Without It Nothing Works." March 21, 2024. Negotiation, Organizations and Markets Research Papers. http://ssrn.com/abstract=1511274.

Jensen, M. C. "Leadership and Leadership Development: An Ontological Approach—Research Summary—Faculty & Research."

March 5, 2024. Harvard Business School. https://www.hbs.edu/faculty/Pages/ item.aspx?research=6811.

Karpman, S. "The History of the Drama Triangle." March 4, 2024. Karpman Drama Triangle. https://karpmandramatriangle.com/pdf/thenewdramatriangles.pdf.

Kassin, S. M. *Psychology*. Pearson/Prentice Hall, 2024.

Kessler, Andy. "The Future Isn't What It Used to Be." Wall Street Journal, June 16, 2019.

Kierkegaard, S. and B. H. Kirmmse. *The Sickness Unto Death: A New Translation*. Liverlight Publishing Corporation, a division of W. W. Norton & Company, Inc., 2024.

Klaas, Brian. *Fluke: Chance, Chaos, and Why Everything We Do Matters.* New York: Scribner, 2024.

Knerl, L. "When Was the Fax Invented." March 21, 2024. HP® Tech Takes. https://www.hp.com/us-en/shop/tech-takes/when-wasfax-invented.

Koestler, A. *The Ghost in the Machine, second printing, unabridged.* Pan Books, 1971.

Kruse, K. "What Is Leadership?" March 25, 2024. Forbes. https://www.forbes.com/ sites/kevinkruse/2013/04/09/what-is-leadership/?sh=1301aba5b90c.

Laloux, F. *Reinventing Organizations: A Guide to Creating Organizations Inspired by the Next Stage of Human Consciousness.* Nelson Parker, 2014.

LaRoche, G., and J. Cohen. *The 7 Laws of Enough: Cultivating a Life of Sustainable Abundance.* Parallax Press, 2018.

Lawrence, T. E. *Seven Pillars of Wisdom.* Jonathan Cape, 1925.

Machiavelli, N., and T. Parks. *The Prince.* Penguin Books, 2014.

Malandro, L. *Fearless Leadership.* McGraw-Hill Education, 2023.

McDaniel, JoBeth. "Weaponized Empathy: The impulse to look out for other people can be hijacked to spread confusion and misinformation." April 28, 2023. https://www.openmindmag.org/articles/weaponized-empathy.

"McDonald's Is Lovin' Its Turnaround." April 3, 2024. *Forbes.* https://www.forbes.com/2004/12/09/ cx_pp_1209overachiever.html#:~:text=To%20do%20that%2C%20it%20wants,open%20location s%20at%20breakneck%20speed.

Mulhall, *S. Routledge Philosophy Guidebook to Heidegger and Being and Time.* Routledge, 2013.

Murray, W. H. *The Scottish Himalayan Expedition.* Dent, 1951.

Nixon, T. *Work With Source, Realize Big Ideas, Organize For Emergence, and Work Artfully with Money.* Tom Nixon LTD, 2021.

Painter, N. I. *The History of White People.* W.W. Norton & Company, 2010.

Pascarella, P., V. Dibianca, and L. Gioja. "The Power of Being Responsible." *Industry Week,* December, 1988.

Perls, F., R. E. Hefferline, and P. Goodman. *Gestalt Therapy: Excitement and Growth in the Human Personality,* 24th printing. Dell, 1951.

Perry, C. "The Jungian Shadow." *Society of Analytical Psychology.* March 4, 2024. The Jungian Shadow. https://www.thesap.org.uk/articles-on-jungian-psychology-2/aboutanalysis-and-therapy/the-shadow/.

Pink, D. H. Drive: *The Surprising Truth about What Motivates Us.* Penguin Group US, 2011.

"Purpose, Vision, and the Southwest Way." April 3, 2024. Southwest Airlines. https:// www.southwestairlinesinvestorrelations.com/our-company/purpose-vision-and-the-southwestway.

Quote by Johann Wolfgang von Goethe. April 26, 2024. Goodreads. https:// www.goodreads.com/quotes/115719-dream-no-small-dreams-for-they-have-no-power-to.

Razeto-Barry, P. "Autopoiesis 40 Years Later. A Review and a Reformulation." *Orig Life Evol Biosph* 42, (2012): 543–567. doi:https://doi.org/10.1007/s11084-012-9297-y.

Razeto-Barry, Pablo. "Autopoiesis 40 Years Later. A Review and a Reformulation." *Orig Life Evol Biosph* 42, (2012): 543–567. doi:https://doi.org/10.1007/s11084-012-9297-y.

"Reengineering the Hot New Managing Tool: The Radical Redesign of Business Processes Is Powerful—And All the FAD. But It's Not for Everyone, and Sometimes It Fails to Deliver. Here's How to Make It Succeed." March 16, 2024. CNNMoney. http://money.cnn.com/magazines/fortune/ fortune_archive/1993/08/23/78237/index.htm.

Reich, C. "On Power by Charles Reich." March 28, 2024. Reality and Mind. https:// realityandmind.wordpress.com/2017/09/17/on-power-by-charles-reich/?trk=article-ssr-frontendpulse_little-text-block.

"Results Do Not Equal No Results Plus Excuses (R ≠ NR + e)." April 5, 2024. 100 Small Things. https://www.100smallthings.com.au/results-not-equal-no-results-plus-excuses/.

Robertson, B. J. *Holacracy: The New Management System for a Rapidly Changing World*. Henry Holt and Company, 2015.

Ryan, J. "Foreword by John Ryan, CEO, Farm Credit Canada." *Say It Right the First Time*. McGraw Hill, 2003.

Sachs, Mendel. *Ideas of the Theory of Relativity*. New York: Wiley-Interscience, 1974.

Searle, J. R. *Speech Acts*. New York, 1976.

Searle, J. R. *Speech Acts: An Essay in the Philosophy of Language*. Cambridge University Press, 1992.

Soskin, R. *Metamorphosis: Astonishing Insect Transformations*. Bloomsbury Publishing PLC, 2015.

Sullivan, Walter. "The Einstein Papers: A Man of Many Parts." *New York Times*, March 29, 1972.

Syed, M. *Black Box Thinking: Why Most People Never Learn from Their Mistakes—But Some Do*. Portfolio Penguin, 2016.

Talbot, Michael. *Beyond the Quantum*. New York: Bantam Books, 1986.

Tannen, D. *You Just Don't Understand: Women and Men in Conversation*. Virago Press, 1995.

Tarakci, M., et al. "Heroes or Villains? Recasting Middle Management Roles, Processes, and Behaviors." *Journal of Management Studies* 60, no. 7, (2023): 1663–1683. doi:10.1111/ joms.12989.

Taylor, F. W. *Scientific Management: Comprising Shop Management, the Principles of Scientific Management*. Harper, 1911.

Taylor, F. W. "Frederick W. Taylor—Hardly a Competent Workman Can Be..." March 16, 2024. https://www.brainyquote.com/quotes/frederick_w_taylor_207405.

Taylor, Jill Bolte. *My Stroke of Genius*. New York: Penguin, 2008.

Tennyson, Alfred. *In Memoria*m. London: Edward Moxon, 1850.

Trungpa, C., and J. L. Lief. (2010) *The Heart of the Buddha: Entering the Tibetan Buddhist Path*. Shambhala, 2010.

Von Goethe, Johann Wolfgang. "All Poetry," Goethe Information and Sources, January 19, 2025, https://www.allpoetry.com

Vonnegut, Kurt. *Deadeye Dick*. Delacorte Press, 1982.

Watts, A. W. *In My Own Way*. Pantheon Books, 1972.

"Welcome to Costco Customer Service: What Is Costco's Return Policy?" April 5, 2024. https://customerservice.costco.

com/app/answers/answer_view/a_id/1191/~/what-iscostco%E2%80%99s-return-policy%3F.

Wilkie, D. "Workplace Gossip: What Crosses the Line?" March 21, 2024. Welcome to SHRM. https://www.shrm.org/topics-tools/news/employee-relations/work-place-gossipcrossesline#:~:text=Some%20negative%20consequences%20of%20workplace,is%20and%20isn't%20f act.

Yohn, D. L. "Company Culture is Everyone's Responsibility," a reprint. *Harvard Business Review*. doi:https://hbr.org/2021/02/company-culture-is-everyones-responsibility.

Zezelj, F. "Why Are Railroad Tracks Constructed in the Width that They Are?" April 24,2024. Quora. https://www.quora.com/Why-were-railroad-tracks-constructed-in-the-widththat-they-were. I am grateful to Dr. Zezelj for posting this amusing formulation on Quora in answer to a question.

Zukav, Gary. *The Dancing Wu Li Masters: An Overview of the New Physics*. New York: William Morrow and Company, 1979.

Ōno, T., and N. Bodek. *Toyota Production System: Beyond Large-Scale Production*. Productivity Press, 1988.

ENDNOTES

[i] Klaas, Brian, Fluke: Chance, Chaos, and Why Everything We Do Matters. 2024 Scribner, New York 2

[ii] S. M. Kassin, *Psychology* (Pearson/Prentice Hall, 2004).

[iii] From Ideas of the Theory of Relativity by Mendel Sachs, 1974 (emphasis added)

[iv] Zukav, Gary. *The Dancing Wu Li Masters: An Overview of the New Physics* (William Morrow and Company, 1979).

[v] Michael Talbot, Beyond the Quantum (1986).

[vi] C. Trungpa and J. L. Lief, *The Heart of the Buddha: Entering the Tibetan Buddhist Path* (Shambhala, 2010).

[vii] J. L. Austin, *How To Do Things with Words: The William James Lectures Delivered at Harvard University In 1955* (Oxford University Press, 2009).

[viii] John Richard Searle, *Speech Acts: An Essay in the Philosophy of Language* (Cambridge University Press, 1969).

[ix] F. Flores, "Conversations for Action and Collected Essays: Instilling a Culture of Commitment in Working Relationships." Createspace (2013).

[x] Jill Bolte Taylor, *My Stroke of Genius* (Penguin, 2008).

xi D. Goleman, *Emotional Intelligence* (Bantam, 1995).

xii M. Heidegger, *Being and Time* (Harper Perennial, 2008).

xiii M. Heidegger, *What Is Called Thinking?* (Harper & Row, 1968) 76–77.

xiv Albert Einstein, letter written in 1950, quoted in Walter Sullivan, "The Einstein Papers: A Man of Many Parts," *New York Times*, March 29, 1972.

xv Tennyson, Alfred, In Memoriam (Edward Moxon, 1850).

xvi Ibid

xvii E. Berne, *What Do You Say After You Say Hello?* (Grove Press, 1972).

xviii Thomas Hübl and Julie Jordan Avritt, *Healing Collective Trauma* (Sounds True, 2020).

xix J. H. Flavell, *The Developmental Psychology of Jean Piaget* (Van Nostrand, 1963) 85.

xx Thomas Hübl and Julie Jordan Avritt, *Healing Collective Trauma* (Sounds True, 2020).

xxi Dispenza, Joe. *Becoming Supernatural: How Common People are Doing the Uncommon*. Carlsbad, California : Hay House, Inc., 2019.

xxii S. Karpman, "The History of the Drama Triangle," Karpman Drama Triangle, 2005, https://karpmandramatriangle.com/pdf/thenewdramatriangles.pdf.

xxiii E. Berne, "Games People Play," Puffin (2010).

xxiv C. Perry, "The Jungian Shadow," Society of Analytical Psychology, 2015, https://www.thesap.org.uk/articles-on-jungian-psychology-2/about-analysisand-therapy/the-shadow/.

xxv B. Brown, "Adding Shame, Guilt, Humiliation, Embarrassment…," 2020, https:// brenebrown.com/wp-content/uploads/2021/09/Integration-Ideas_Emotional-Vocabulary_092221-1.pdf.

xxvi M. Heidegger, original edition of *Being and Time* (Must Have Books, 2021). Quotation includes author-added emphasis.

xxvii Quote by Richard Bach, October 13, 2022, LinkedIn. https://www.linkedin.com/pulse/argue-yourlimitations-sure-enough-theyre-#:~:text=I%20had%20concluded%20that%20there,enough%20they're%20yours.%22.

xxviii M. C. Jensen, "Leadership and Leadership Development: An Ontological Approach—Research Summary," Harvard Business School, June 2009, https://www.hbs.edu/faculty/Pages/ item.aspx?research=6811.

xxix V. E. Frankl, H. S. Kushner, and W. J. Winslade, *Man's Search for Meaning* (Beacon Press, 2006).

xxx S. R. Covey, "First Things First: To Live, to Love, to Learn, to Leave a Legacy" (Covey Leadership Center, 1994).

xxxi F. Perls, R. E. Hefferline, and P. Goodman, "Gestalt Therapy: Excitement and Growth in the Human Personality" (Dell, 1951).

xxxii D. Goleman, *Emotional Intelligence* (Bloomsbury, 1996).

xxxiii Jana Wilson, "Sideview of brain highlighting amygdala". Figure 6. 2024 xxxiv John Richard Searle, *Speech Acts: An Essay in the Philosophy of Language* (Cambridge University Press, 1969).

xxxv F. Flores, Conversations for Action and Collected Essays: Instilling a Culture of Commitment in Working Relationships (Createspace, 2013).

xxxvi There have been many variations on this idea—one of the first was in T. Ōno and N. Bodek's *Toyota Production System: Beyond Large-Scale Production* (Productivity Press, 1988).

xxxvii L. Malandro, *Fearless Leadership* (McGraw-Hill Education, 2023).

xxxviii T. Goss, *Last Word on Power* (Rosetta Books, 2010).

xxxix S. Kierkegaard, and B. H. Kirmmse, *The Sickness Unto Death: A New Translation* (Liverlight Publishing Corporation, a division of W. W. Norton & Company, Inc., 2024). Quotation used includes author-added emphasis and paraphrasing.

xl Quote by Michelangelo Buonarroti, Goodreads, https:// www. goodreads.com/quotes/10320211-i-created-a-vision-of-david-in-my-mindand#:~:text=Sign%20Up%20Now-,I%20created%20 a%20vision%20of%20David%20in%20my %20mind%20 and,everything%20that%20was%20not%20David.

xli S. Mulhall, *Routledge Philosophy Guidebook to Heidegger and "Being and Time,"* second edition (Routledge, 2005), 15.

xlii W. Erhard, "Epistemological and Contextual Contributions of EST to General Systems Theory," Symposium on Evolving Trends in General Systems Theory and the Future of the Family, 1976.

xliii W. H. Murray, *The Scottish Himalayan Expedition* (Dent, 1951).

xliv Rayona Sharpnack, personal communication.

xlv W. Erhard, "Werner Erhard—A World that Works For Everyone About You, Make a Difference," YouTube, March 12, 2024, https://www.youtube.com/watch?v=dTkGZq6mhJI.

xlvii R. S. de Ropp, *The Master Game* (Delacorte, 1968).

xlviii e.e. cummings, *A Miscellany*, edited by G. J. Firmage (Liveright Publishing Corporation, a division of W. W. Norton & Company, 2018).

xlix Frederick Winslow Taylor, *The Principles of Scientific Management* (Harper & Brothers, 1911).

l Ibid., 7.

li F. W. Taylor, "Frederick W. Taylor—Hardly a Competent Workman Can Be…," Brainy Quotes, March 16, 2024, https://www.brainyquote.com/quotes/frederick_w_taylor_207405.

lii M. Friedman, "Milton Friedman: The Profit Doctrine," 2016, 55–77, doi:10.2307/j.ctt1jktsbd.9.

liii K. Harbott, "The History of Hierarchies," Agile Centre, March 16, 2024, https:// www.agilecentre.com/resources/article/the-history-of-hierarchies/. Much of the preceding section is based on Harbott's work.

liv "Reengineering the Hot New Managing Tool: The Radical Redesign of Business Processes Is Powerful—And All the FAD, But It's Not for Everyone, and Sometimes It Fails to Deliver. Here's How to Make It Succeed," CNNMoney, March 16, 2024, http://money.cnn.com/magazines/ fortune/fortune_archive/1993/08/23/78237/index.htm.

[lv] M. Syed, "Black Box Thinking: Why Most People Never Learn from Their Mistakes—But Some Do," Portfolio Penguin, 2016.

[lvi] L. Knerl, "When Was the Fax Invented: HP® Tech Takes," HP® Tech Takes, March 21, 2024, https://www.hp.com/us-en/shop/tech-takes/when-wasfax-invented.

[lvii] The following draws are from P. Pascarella, V. Dibianca, and L. Gioja's "The Power of Being Responsible," *Industry Week*, December 5, 1988.

[lviii] L. Malandro, L. *Fearless Leadership* (McGraw-Hill Education, 2023) 267.

[lix] M. C. Jensen, "Integrity: Without It Nothing Works," Negotiation, Organizations and Markets Research Papers, March 21, 2024, http://ssrn.com/abstract=1511274.

[lx] C. Clark, "Fundamental of the Week #3: Speak Straight, Respectfully," SPEAK STRAIGHT, RESPECTFULLY, March 21, 2024, https://www.momentumconsulting.com/blog/ fundamental-week-3-speak-straight-respectfully?rq=communication.

[lxi] Malandro, L Ibid., chapter 6.

[lxii] Malandro, L Ibid., 158.

[lxiii] See, for example, D. Wilkie, "Workplace Gossip: What Crosses the Line?", March 21, 2024, https:// www.shrm.org/topics-tools/news/employee-relations/workplace-gossip-crossesline#:~:text=Some%20negative%20consequences%20of%20workplace,is%20and%20isn't%20f act.

[lxiv] K. Kruse, "What is Leadership?", Forbes, March 25, 2024, https:// www.forbes.com/sites/kevinkruse/2013/04/09/what-is-leadership/?sh=1301aba5b90c.

[lxv] P. F. Drucker, *The Essential Drucker: The Best of Sixty Years of Peter Drucker's Essential Writings on Management* (Harper, 2014).

[lxvi] G. Boudreaux, "Peter Drucker's Continuing Relevance for Electric Cooperatives," Management Quarterly, 4th edition, (2005) 15, 18–32.

[lxvii] D. R. Hawkins, *Power vs. Force: The Hidden Determinants of Human Behavior* (Hay House, Inc., 2014).

[lxviii] G. LaRoche and J. Cohen, *The 7 Laws of Enough: Cultivating a Life of Sustainable Abundance* (Parallax Press, 2018).

[lxix] C. Reich, "On Power by Charles Reich," Reality and Mind, March 28, 2024, https:// realityandmind.wordpress. com/2017/09/17/on-power-by-charles-reich/?trk=article-ssr-frontendpulse_little-text-block.

[lxx] Call them CEO, managing director, or executive director, it doesn't matter—I'm talking about the person with whom the buck stops and who has been given the task of running the organization by the board, owners, shareholders, etc.

[lxxi] R. Soskin, *Metamorphosis: Astonishing Insect Transformations* (Bloomsbury Publishing PLC, 2015).

[lxxii] T. Nixon, T. *Work with Source: Realize Big Ideas, Organize for Emergence and Work Artfully with Money* (Tom Nixon LTD, 2021).

[lxxiii] For example, M. Tarakci, et al's 2023 article "Heroes or Villains? Recasting Middle Management Roles, Processes, and Behaviours," *Journal of Management Studies 60, no. 7* (2023) 1663–1683, doi:10.1111/joms.12989.

lxxiv For a comprehensive look at important biases that interfere with thinking, see R. Dobelli's *The Art of Thinking Clearly* (Hodder and Stoughton, 2014).

lxxv E. Carpenter, "The Eskimo Language," *ETC: A Review of General Semantics 25*, no. 4 (1968) 467–473, doi:https://www.jstor.org/stable/42574505.

lxxvi McDonald's is Lovin' its Turnaround (2013) Forbes. Available at: https://www.forbes.com/2004/12/09/cx_pp_1209overachiever.html#:~:text=To%20do%20that%2C%20it20wants,open%20locaons%20at%20breakneck%20speed. (Accessed: 03 April 2024).

lxxvii Elmore, B.J. (2023) Country capitalism how corporations from the American South Remade Our Economy and the Planet. Chapel Hill: University of North Carolina Press.

lxxviii Purpose, vision, and the southwest way (2024) – Southwest Airlines. Available at: https://www.southwestairlinesinvestorrelaons.com/our-company/purpose-vision-and-the-southwest-way (Accessed: 03 April 2024).

lxxix Ibid. Employees' Promise

lxxx "What Is Costco's Return Policy?" Costco Customer Service, April 5, 2024, https://customerservice.costco.com/app/answers/answer_view/a_id/1191/~/what-iscostco%E2%80%99s-return-policy%3F.

lxxxi J. B. Izzo, *Stepping up: How Taking Responsibility Changes Everything* (Berrett-Koehler Publishers, Inc., 2020).

lxxxii L. Malandro, *Fearless Leadership* (McGraw-Hill Education, 2023).

lxxxiii For example, see https://www.100smallthings.com.au/results-not-equal-no-resultsplus-excuses/.

lxxxiv G. Hamel and C. K. *Prahalad, Strategic Intent* (Harvard Business Review, 2010).

lxxxv D. L. Yohn, "Company Culture Is Everyone's Responsibility," a preprint, Harvard Business Review, 2021, doi:https://hbr.org/2021/02/company-culture-is-everyonesresponsibility.

lxxxvi T. Nixon, T. *Work with Source: Realize Big Ideas, Organize for Emergence And Work Artfully With Money.* Erscheinungsort nicht ermittelbar: workwithsource (2021).

lxxxvii Ibid., 21.

lxxxviii F. Laloux, *Reinventing Organizations: A Guide to Creating Organizations Inspired by the Next Stage of Human Consciousness* (Nelson Parker, 2014).

lxxxix https://en.wikipedia.org/wiki/Cultural_practice#Examples.

xc I learned the importance of cultural practices as applied to organizational transformation from Dr. Loretta Malandro during my work with her. I am indebted to her for this idea and much of what follows.

xci "Foreword by John Ryan, CEO, Farm Credit Canada," *Say It Right the First Time* special edition printing, by Dr. Loretta Malandro (McGraw-Hill, 2005).

xcii Ibid., 29–31.

xciii W. H. Murray, *The Scottish Himalayan Expedition* (Dent, 1951).

xciv P. Drucker, *Practice of Management* (Harper & Row, 1954).

xcv R. Babineaux and J. D. Krumboltz, *Fail Fast, Fail Often: How Losing Can Help You Win* (Jeremy P. Tarcher/Penguin, 2013).

xcvi Machiavelli, N. and Parks, T. (2014) The Prince. London: Penguin Books.

xcvii F. Zezelj, "Why Are Railroad Tracks Constructed in the Width That They Are?" Quora, April 24, 2024, https://www.quora.com/Why-were-railroad-tracks-constructed-in-the-widththat-they-were. I am grateful to Dr. Zezelj for posting this amusing formulation on Quora in answer to a question.

xcviii D. H. Pink, Drive: *The Surprising Truth about What Motivates Us* (Penguin Group US, 2011).

xcix Pink, op. cit., 3.

c Vonnegut, Kurt. *Deadeye Dick.* New York: Delacorte Press, 1982.

ci C. Dweck, "What Having a 'Growth Mindset' Actually Means," Harvard Business Review, April 25, 2024, https://hbr.org/2016/01/what-having-a-growth-mindset-actuallymeans.

cii E. M. Gurowitz, Inclusion, the Role of Leadership: Why We Are Separate, Why We Need to Come Together (Halo Publishing International, 2019).

ciii N. I. Painter, *The History of White People* (W.W. Norton & Company, 2010).

civ C. Gilligan, *Joining the Resistance* (Polity Press, 2013).

cv D. Tannen, *You Just Don't Understand: Women and Men in Conversation* (Virago Press, 1995).

cvi A. Comte and H. Martineau, *The Positive Philosophy of Auguste Comte* (Kegan Paul, Trench, Trübner & Co, 1853).

cvii B. J. Robertson, *Holacracy: The New Management System for a Rapidly Changing World* (Henry Holt and Company, 2015).

cviii A. Koestler, *The Ghost in the Machine, unabridged, second printing* (Pan Books, 1971).

cix Robertson, op. cit.

cx A. Groth, "Zappos Has Quietly Backed Away from Holacracy," Yahoo! Finance, April 25, 2024, https://Finance.Yahoo.Com/News/Zappos-Quietly-backed-awayholacracy-090102533.html.

cxi https://mkpusa.org/org-charts/.

cxii F. Laloux, *Reinventing Organizations: A Guide to Creating Organizations Inspired by the Next Stage of Human Consciousness* (Nelson Parker, 2014).

cxiii R. Bly, *Iron John: A Book About Men* — 25th Anniversary Edition (Da Capo Press, 2015).

cxiv J. Campbell, *The Hero With A Thousand Faces* (Joseph Campbell Foundation, 2020).

cxv G. Bateson, et al., "Toward a Theory of Schizophrenia," *Behavioral Science* 1 (1956) 251-254.

cxvi Andy Kessler, "The Future Isn't What It Used to Be," *Wall Street Journal,* June 16, 2019.

cxvii All butterfly references are from: (1) "How Does a Caterpillar Turn Into a Butterfly?" *Discover Wildlife*, August 31,2024, https://www.discoverwildlife.com/animal-facts/insectsinvertabrates/how-does-a-caterpillar-turn-into-a-butterfly; (2) "Butterfly Life Cycle for Educators" University of Florida, August 31,2024, https://www.floridamuseum.ufl.edu/educators/resource/butterfly-life-cycle/; and (3)

"Butterfly Metamorphosis," American Museum of Natural History, August 31, 2024, https://www.amnh.org/exhibitions/butterflies/metamorphosis.

cxviii A.W. Watts, *In My Own Way* (Pantheon Books, 1972), xii

cxix Pablo Razeto-Barry, "Autopoiesis 40 Years Later. A Review and a Reformulation," *Original Life Evil Biosph* 42 (2012): 543-567, doi:https://doi.org/10.1007/ s11084-012-9297-y.

cxx M. Heidegger, *What Is Called Thinking?* (Harper & Row, 1968).

cxxi https://www.openmindmag.org/articles/weaponized-empathy.

cxxii MIT Researcher Cameron Martel, cited in *Open Minds magazine* (op. cit.).

cxxiii https://www.forbes.com/sites/traversmark/2024/06/19/2-ways-narcissistsweaponize-empathy-for-personal-gain-by-a-psychologist/.

cxxiv https://zocalopublicsquare.org/2017/07/17/weaponization-empathy-hyperconnected-world/inquiries/small-science/.

cxxv G. Bateson, *Steps to an Ecology of Mind: Collected Essays in Anthropology, Psychology, Evolution and Epistemology* (Intertext Books, 1972).

cxxvi A quote by Johann Wolfgang von Goethe (no date) Goodreads. Available at: https://www.goodreads.com/quotes/115719-dream-no-small-dreams-for-they-have-no-power-to (Accessed: 26 April 2024).

cxxvii Lawrence, T.E. (1925) Seven Pillars of Wisdom. London, UK: Jonathan Cape.

cxxviii Vonnegut, Kurt. Deadeye Dick. New York: Delacorte Press, 1982.

cxxix Goss, Tracy. *The Last Word on Power: Executive Re-Invention for Leaders Who Must Make the Impossible Happen*. New York: Currency Doubleday, 1995.

cxxx Brené Brown, "The Power of Vulnerability," TEDxHouston, June 2010, video, 20:04, https://www.ted.com/talks/brene_brown_the_power_of_vulnerability.

cxxxi Finkelstein, N.H. (1991) Theodor Herzl: Architect of a Nation. Minneapolis, MN, MN: Lerner Publications Co.

LET'S CONNECT

Find out more about Edward M. Gurowitz Ph.D.

Email: egurowitz@gurowitz.com

LinkedIn: Ed Gurowitz

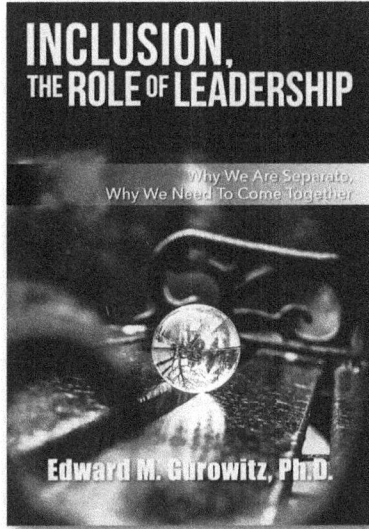

Too often, men are seen as enemies of others' advancement or, at best, as bystanders. However, in business and in life men have advantages and power and can be powerful allies. This book reviews the case for inclusion and allyship, outlines what gets in the way of that, and provides tools for men to use their power for the good of all--for their businesses, their relationships, and themselves.

Inclusion, The Role of Leadership: Why We Are Separate, Why We Need to Come Together

ISBN Hardcover: 978-1-61244-789-6
ISBN Paperback: 978-1-61244-768-1
Hardcover Price: $20.95
Paperback Price: $12.95
Page Count: 112 pages

www.ingramcontent.com/pod-product-compliance
Lightning Source LLC
Chambersburg PA
CBHW072140270326
41931CB00010B/1825